WHO SAYS WINNERS NEVER LOSE?

Profiting from Life's Painful Detours

by Diana Kruger

Aglow Publications
A Ministry of Women's Aglow Fellowship, Int'l.
P.O. Box 1548
Lynnwood, WA 98046-1558
USA

Cover design by David Marty

Unless otherwise noted, all scripture quotations in this publication are from the Holy Bible, New International Version. Copyright ©1973, 1978, 1984, International Bible Society. Other versions are abbreviated as follows: KJV (King James Version), TLB (The Living Bible).

©Copyright 1990, Diana Kruger. Published by Aglow Publications, A Ministry of Women's Aglow Fellowship, Int'l., Lynnwood, WA, USA. All rights reserved. Except for brief quotations for review purposes, no part of this book may be reproduced in any form or by any electronic or mechanical means without prior permission in writing from the publisher. Printed in the United States of America.

ISBN 0-932305-79-2

Because losing them sent me on my most painful detours where I learned my most valuable lessons, this book is dedicated to the memory of my son, Mallon Ronald Kruger, and my father, Philip David Savage.

Introduction

Years ago, I heard about a woman who unknowingly knocked a valuable brooch off her dressing table into a wastebasket. As she sat combing her hair, she heard the garbage truck coming down the alley, realized she had forgotten to put out the garbage, and grabbed the wastebasket on her way out.

"Just in time, lady," the man told her, tossing the contents into the truck.

When she was ready to put on the brooch, she couldn't find it anywhere. Realizing what must have happened, she called the disposal company and learned the truck had just emptied its load at the landfill.

Donning old clothes and rubber gloves, the wealthy woman went to the dump and began to comb through the garbage. Day after day, she picked through chicken bones, dirty diapers, used tissue, cigarette butts—all in a fruitless search for her missing brooch.

The woman's loss affected her deeply even though the piece of jewelry was merely a possession. Some would say it wasn't worth grieving over—but its loss changed the woman's living pattern.

For one couple in the Bible, losing all their possessions was only the beginning of their troubles. In one day, they plunged from their position as the richest people in the country to that of penniless paupers. Also on that day, their ten children were killed in a freak accident. A short time later, the husband came down with a disfiguring skin disease. Something in the woman snapped and she spewed anger at God.

In spite of their pain, they did not receive consolation from others. Three of the man's closest friends insisted that he must be secretly sinning or he wouldn't have lost

Who Says Winners Never Lose?

everything. Everyone who heard about the woman's outburst branded her as evil.

Those all-time losers were, of course, Job and his wife. They experienced loss of possessions, loss of loved ones, loss of health, and loss of dignity and other intangibles; and she experienced, at least temporarily, the loss of faith in God. People today, no matter how "good" they are, can experience loss in the same categories. We will study these losses in detail, examine the basic reasons why we lose, and discuss why God sometimes allows loss.

An important part of recovery is understanding the grief process—a process about which many Christians have distorted views. We'll look at the barriers to recovery, find out how loss can actually become gain, and sum it all up with examples of restoration, comfort, and hope from scripture.

Nearly everyone suffers loss at one time or another, but these painful detours need not maroon anyone at the roadside. God provides instruction manuals, road signs, even roving mechanics to help us if we will only look for them.

I hope this book will serve as one of those helps.

—Diana Kruger

Contents

PART I
Over the Cliff

Chapter 1	What is Loss?	11
Chapter 2	What Does Our Map Say?	19
Chapter 3	Those Hairpin Curves	31
Chapter 4	What About the Guardrails?	43

PART II
The Treasures We Lose

Chapter 5	Loss of Possessions	57
Chapter 6	Loss of Loved Ones	65
Chapter 7	Loss of Health	75
Chapter 8	Loss of Dignity and Other Intangibles	85
Chapter 9	Loss of Faith in God	97

PART III
Search and Rescue

Chapter 10	Climbing the Steep Trail Out	109
Chapter 11	Nursing Our Wounds	119
Chapter 12	Discovering the Gold	129
Chapter 13	Resuming the Journey	139

Source Notes 149

Support Group Leader's Guide 155

Part I
Over the Cliff

1

What Is Loss?

My alarm clock chimed "Oh, What a Beautiful Morning." Even before I opened my eyes, an enormous weight of loss slammed down on me like a sledge hammer.

Every morning was the same. When I awoke, I remembered. For weeks, ever since our son had died of liver cancer on his first birthday, bereavement engulfed me like a hot, smothering blanket.

I couldn't escape the physical reminders. My body still produced milk, and I was swollen and tender. Bags puffed around my eyes. Facial tissue had rubbed my nose raw. At night, I'd awaken to listen for his cries—and crumple in sobs when I remembered I would never again hear my baby's voice.

Deep inside me throbbed a gaping hole with bleeding edges. My son had been ripped from my grasp, and I felt

Who Says Winners Never Lose?

empty and limp from the struggle.

Thousands of babies die every year, and their deaths do not affect me as my son's did. Why did Mallon's death cause me to suffer so? Because I lost him. His death was a loss to me.

WHAT IS LOSS?

I cringe when I hear people say, "As Christians, we don't really lose our loved ones. We know right where they are—with Jesus."

Such statements play at semantics. Loss means more than not knowing where something is. Loss is "being deprived of or coming to be without something that one has had." Another definition is "the harm resulting from losing."

Not all loss results in harm. We rejoice when we lose saddlebag thighs, warts on our noses, or hoodlums on a dark street. We work hard to get rid of bad credit ratings. People pay treatment centers a great deal of money in hopes of losing a craving for alcohol or cocaine.

The loss that hurts must necessarily be the loss of something we value—a treasure. Whenever we lose, we feel as if we're plunging into a chasm. As we free-fall through the air, we experience anger and helplessness. In the crash landing, we suffer bruises and breaks. Then we are faced with the choice of wallowing in our misery or climbing the steep trail back to the path. We can look for hidden benefits, or we can remain bitter throughout life.

Whatever our reaction, we will never again be the same after losing a treasure.

Family counselor Ira Tanner says, "There is, I learned, no predictable response to any form of loss. In fact, one man's loss of hair caused him more grief than another's loss of a beloved relative."[1] Personality, age, emotional health,

What is Loss?

timing, previous losses, degree of trust in God—all have a part in determining a person's reaction.

COMPOUND OR COMPENSATE

There is no common denominator among people who experience loss. Loss touches everyone—rich, poor; young, old; American, third-world; brunette, bald. While losing treasures is a common experience, the variety of ways in which people respond either compounds the original loss or compensates for it.

Great-uncle Walter was an independent farmer. Several years ago, he slipped on the ice in front of his home, broke his hip, and lay for hours in freezing weather before a neighbor found him and called an ambulance.

He survived the chill but not his loss of freedom. Whenever Mark and I were in town, we would visit him at the nursing home.

"They didn't set my leg right," he would complain. "Now it's shorter than the other one." After one attempt, he refused to walk with a walker for fear he would fall. His world soon shrank to a nine-by-nine room.

"Why don't you ask a nurse to walk beside you?" I suggested. "Maybe if you tried just one step at first and increased a little every day...."

He had an excuse for every idea and continued to waste away until his death two years later. Uncle Walter allowed his loss to compound until it overcame him.

Joni Eareckson Tada, on the other hand, is a famous example of someone who compensates for her losses. She can't paint with her hands so she holds a brush in her mouth. Her paralysis doesn't limit her singing, speaking, or creative writing abilities, so she uses those in her outreach to hurting people.

Compensation does not make life easy for Joni. Her

Who Says Winners Never Lose?

original loss has never been restored. She must deal with all the frustrations of being a quadriplegic—the humiliation of needing help for personal care, full-time attendants, the prison of paralysis. In addition, fame has brought her the complication of a "fish bowl" life.

Yet Joni is an inspiration to millions because she chooses to compensate for her losses instead of letting her losses compound.

We have the power to choose our response to loss. Life and death can literally hang in the balance of that decision.

TWO RESPONSES

Job and his wife exhibit two differing responses to the same tragic circumstances. Immediately after learning he had lost every bit of wealth, all ten of his children, and nearly all of his servants, Job said, "The Lord gave and the Lord has taken away; may the name of the Lord be praised" (Job 1:21). Scripture says Job did not sin "in what he said," nor "by charging God with wrongdoing."

But after his friends arrived and sat around for a week silently contemplating the situation, Job let loose a barrage of curses against the day of his birth and those who had allowed him to live. He wailed, "I have no peace, no quietness; I have no rest, but only turmoil" (Job 3:26).

God waited while Job and his accusers battled verbally. Then, out of a raging storm with wind, thunder, and lightning for background effect, God put Job in his place by asking him unanswerable questions.

Thoroughly shaken now from any hint of pomposity, Job began, "I know that you can do all things" (Job 42:2), and ended "I despise myself and repent in dust and ashes" (Job 42:6).

Job's wife is famous for telling her husband to curse God and die. I am convinced, however, that we are too quick to

What is Loss?

assume she did it out of an evil heart. Everything that Job lost, she lost too. When he became a pauper, so did she. Her social and financial positions were inseparably linked with her husband's.

She had given birth to those ten children and was as bereaved as Job at their death. In addition to her sorrow, she now bore the stigma of being a childless woman—a despised condition in those days.[2]

Scripture does not record a single complaint from her lips as a result of these staggering blows. It wasn't until Job's health was stricken that she uttered her famous speech, "Curse God and die."

We now know that one of the early stages of grief is anger. Burdened with sudden poverty, bereavement, and added responsibilities in caring almost single-handedly for a sick husband, she no doubt seethed with anger—toward God for letting all this happen and toward herself because she couldn't accept and believe God the same way Job did.

People today react as she did. Harriet Sarnoff Schiff tells of two people who each responded differently to their daughter's death. The father turned completely away from religion, while the mother became more devout than ever. And she never outwardly mourned.

> "Now that Pammy is with God, how can I be sad? It is the most glorious thing that can happen. I only thank Him for taking her so young, before she came to know the pain of this world," said the wife.
>
> Her husband sat, squirming, as his wife expressed herself.
>
> "Damn it," he yelled, "I am getting sick and tired of hearing how great it is that she is dead. It is not great. It stinks. She was beautiful. She was smart. She was my daughter, and I will never be thankful she is dead.

Who Says Winners Never Lose?

What is wrong with you?"

The mother arose with a superior and knowing smile on her face and left the room.

"This is what always happens," said the husband. "She gets up with a smart-aleck look on her face and leaves the room. How can she be grateful, *grateful*, Pammy is dead?"[3]

The man obviously was in great emotional pain. Let us note here that he was not, as is universally suggested about Job's wife, allowed to live merely to be a further temptation to his spouse.

The parish priest came to visit the couple and saw the antagonism between them. He invited the man to the parish office just to talk, "no strings attached." Because the husband saw that the priest was not one to "strew every sentence with 'God will provide' and 'God will make everything all right,' " he agreed.

A friendship developed between the two men that helped diffuse the husband's hostility toward religion, which was his wife's main source of comfort.

For many people, losing a treasure profoundly affects their faith in God one way or another. This reaction results from their concept of God and how he deals with us.

AREAS OF LOSS

Job and his wife illustrate five basic areas in which we suffer loss:
- loss of possessions
- loss of loved ones
- loss of health
- loss of dignity and other intangibles
- loss of faith in God

What is Loss?

The "harm that results from losing" often inflicts great pain. Denial, simplistic answers, or blind acceptance cannot erase that pain.

In this book, we will deal with why we lose, the five areas of loss, the process of recovery, gaining from loss, and comfort and restoration.

When loss bumps us off the edge of the cliff, what we believe about how God deals with us profoundly affects our reactions. Let's examine those beliefs in the next chapter.

TIME TO CONSIDER

1. Have you ever lost a treasure? How did it affect you?

2. If you have ever compounded or compensated for a loss, describe how.

3. What choice or choices made the difference between compounding and compensating?

2

What Does Our Map Say?

When we probe the core of people's belief systems, we generally find three basic assumptions:
- If we are righteous, God will bless and protect us.
- If we suffer, it is because we have sinned.
- If we sin, God will punish us.

A man wins twenty-three million dollars in the lottery. Friends and neighbors gather around and clap him on the back. "Lucky guy!" one remarks. "You sure must live right!"

A husband and wife get behind in the rent. They miss too many car payments, and the vehicle is repossessed. Just when the wife finds a secretarial job, she breaks her arm. That evening, the refrigerator quits. "What did we do to deserve this?" they ask.

People respond in this manner because of how they think

Who Says Winners Never Lose?

God deals with people. Live right, and life will be smooth; blow it, and God will zap you. Let's examine these assumptions.

1. *If we are righteous, will God always bless and protect us?* Because Abraham lived a godly life, God promised him many descendants (some of them kings) who would inherit the land of Canaan. God blessed Abraham with wealth and safeguarded his family many times.

Centuries later, God promised the entire nation of Israel that he would show mercy "unto thousands of them that love me and keep my commandments" (Deut. 5:10 KJV).

In reminding a new generation of Israelites of the law, Moses said, "Carefully follow the terms of this covenant, so that you may prosper in everything you do" (Deut. 29:9).

Non-Jewish people who try to claim these promises should note that they were given specifically to Abraham and his Hebrew descendents.

Other scripture, however, applies to the godly no matter what their bloodlines. "Surely I know that it shall be well with them that fear God" (Eccles. 8:12 KJV). "A good man obtains favor from the Lord" (Prov. 12:2). "The name of the Lord is a strong tower; the righteous run to it and are safe" (Prov. 18:10).

In the New Testament, Jesus promised his followers, "If you remain in me and my words remain in you, ask whatever you wish, and it will be given you" (John 15:7). In the Sermon on the Mount, he assured them of the heavenly Father's care: "But seek first his kingdom and his righteousness, and all these things will be given to you as well" (Matt. 6:33).

So we see scripture that supports the belief, *if we are righteous, God will always bless and protect us*. On the other hand, we find plenty of exceptions.

Hebrews 11:35–39 talks about saints who were righteous

What Does Our Map Say?

and yet suffered all sorts of horrors. They were faithful "yet none of them received what had been promised" (v. 39).

John the Baptist never got out of prison alive and, in death, received no respect. To fulfill the wishes of a saucy dance girl, his head was paraded on a platter through Herod's court.

While active in missionary service, Paul was imprisoned, whipped five times, beaten three times, stoned, shipwrecked three times, and adrift once for twenty-four hours on the open sea. He was in danger from rivers, bandits, his own people, foreigners, and enemies. He went without sleep, food, warmth, and clothing (2 Cor. 11:23–27).

A number of years ago, while veteran missionaries Jay and Angeline Tucker were in the United States on furlough, the Belgian Congo (now Zaire) erupted in rebellion. Instead of listening to friends who warned them to wait until the unrest subsided, they committed themselves to God's protection and returned to their missionary work.

Two days before Thanksgiving, 1964, Jay Tucker was clubbed to death. The next day his body was hauled fifty miles into the area of Nganga and thrown into the crocodile-infested Bomokandi River.

When news of the attack reached friends back home, people could hardly believe it. Why would something like this happen to such a fine missionary family? Why hadn't God protected this dedicated man serving him in a remote corner of the world? Where was he when the Tuckers had cried out for protection?

Clearly we must dig a little deeper for answers to these questions or we run the risk of concluding that God is powerless or does not care. What are the hidden factors in unexplained circumstances such as this?

2. *If we suffer, is it because we have sinned?* The infant prince barely breathed. A small group of men moved

Who Says Winners Never Lose?

quietly past the nursery and out into the already hot morning. As they approached the king stretched on the ground, one knelt and asked him to join them them for dinner.

The king shook his head. "Oh God!" he cried. "Spare my son! Oh Lord, have mercy, I beg you."

As the king remained on his face in the courtyard, fasting and praying throughout the week, death came daily nearer to the infant. On the seventh day, the baby died.

The attendants couldn't decide how to break the news to the baby's father. "He was so upset while the child was still alive, what harm might he do to himself if we tell him the child is dead?" they whispered among themselves.

But when the king learned of his son's death, he rose slowly, washed, changed his clothes, and sat down to eat. The attendants stood aside in shock.

"I wept and fasted while the infant was alive in the event that the Lord would be gracious to me and let the child live," the king explained. "But now that he is dead, I can't bring him back again."

Although he suffered deeply, as bereaved parents do, King David was not tormented with the usual question of why it had happened. Shortly after his son's birth, a prophet of God had announced that the baby would die as punishment for David's adulterous affair with Bathsheba and because David had choreographed her husband's death.

This account clearly illustrates the second basic assumption many people make about how God deals with us: *If we suffer, it is because we have sinned.*

As they fled from slavery in Egypt, the Israelites provided many illustrations of this principle. One day Moses returned from the mountain where he had received religious instruction from God, only to find the people worshiping a golden calf. As punishment, three thousand people died by the sword and many more suffered from a

What Does Our Map Say?

plague.

Because the people grumbled about their hardships, God consumed some of them with fire. When they whined for meat, God sent another death plague.

God struck Miriam with leprosy when she criticized Moses.

When the Israelites refused to believe God would help them conquer the people of Canaan, he consigned them to forty years in the wilderness.

A yawning chasm swallowed up three rebel leaders, their families, and their belongings. When the people complained about it, another plague swept the camp, killing 14,700. More complaining about living conditions brought a swarm of venomous snakes. For worshipping Baal, twenty-four thousand died of still another plague.

The history of Israel clearly shows us people who suffered because they sinned.

Deuteronomy is packed with verses that say in essence, "Do what's right, and God will bless you. Step out of line and . . . watch out." Even before the law was given, this basic belief was so ingrained in the minds of ancient peoples that when Job's friends were confronted with his tremendous losses, they assumed it was because Job had sinned.

Eliphaz minced no words. "Is it because you are good that he is punishing you? Not at all! It is because of your wickedness! Your sins are endless!" (Job 22:4,5 TLB).

God was not pleased by this. At the end of the book of Job, he turned his attention to Eliphaz. "I am angry with you and with your two friends, for you have not been right in what you have said about me, as my servant Job was" (Job 42:7 TLB).

Jesus' disciples assumed that the man blind from birth was sightless as a direct result of sin.

Who Says Winners Never Lose?

"'Neither this man nor his parents sinned,' said Jesus, 'but this happened so that the work of God might be displayed in his life'" (John 9:3).

Clearly then, all suffering is not the result of sin. The Holy Spirit chose to include Job's story in scripture—along with other narratives—so we could have such assurance.

Yet, as if to remind us that we cannot swing the pendulum too far in that direction, God brings us back on center with his next remark to Eliphaz, telling him to gather animals so Job could offer a burnt offering. "I will accept his prayer on your behalf, and won't destroy you as I should because of your sin" (Job 42:8 TLB).

As always, the key is balance.

3. *If we sin, will God punish us?* At first glance, this seems a restatement of the previous assumption—*If we suffer, it is because we have sinned*. But looking at this belief from a different angle focuses our attention more on God's response and less on that of the sufferer.

Some people seem to view God as a cosmic cop, poised with a giant billy club, waiting to squash the slightest offender.

The account of Ananias and Sapphira in Acts 5:1–11 lends support to this view. When they lied to Peter about how much money they sold some land for, they fell over dead.

"Great fear seized the whole church and all who heard about these events" (v. 11). We can safely assume that for several weeks thereafter, people thought twice before lying.

That's the point. The early church was brand new. Christianity had just been born. Precedents were being set that still guide us two thousand years later. The Holy Spirit knew the church needed a healthy respect for honesty, and Ananias and Sapphira were the first examples to "volunteer."

What Does Our Map Say?

When Israel was a brand-new nation, just emerging from centuries of slavery, God dealt swiftly and harshly with them. He wanted them to learn the rules for their own good. Like stubborn children, they chose to learn the hard way.

Other examples of God's judgment contain the common thread of rebellion. On the other hand, when people were not rebellious but stumbled into sin anyway, God showed patience and mercy.

THE ALL-IMPORTANT MOTIVES

Imagine a mother taking a walk with two small boys. Nicky doesn't look where he is going and trips headfirst into a mud puddle. Does the mother scold him for being naughty? Watch as she wipes the damp hair from his face, comforts his sobs with kisses, and wraps him in her jacket. "Next time you'll watch where you're going," she says.

When they reach the next puddle, Nicky carefully walks around the edge. Christopher, however, deliberately jumps into the middle and gets just as wet as Nicky. Mother does not treat him the same.

"You did that on purpose, Chris. When we get back from our walk, you can't watch television for the rest of the evening."

Achan didn't get a second chance when he buried forbidden battle spoil under his tent. It was a premeditated act—in that crucial "learning the rules" period for Israel.

The difference is motive. As we study examples in the Bible, we see over and over that God is patient with stumbling pilgrims who truly want to do right. Peter's foot-in-mouth syndrome was not caused by rebellion. When he was afraid and denied the Lord, he repented bitterly with tears. And Jesus forgave him.

David committed other sins besides adultery. Each time, he repented. God himself referred to David as "a man after

Who Says Winners Never Lose?

God's own heart" and always gave him another chance.

God deals severely with rebelliousness—especially when he is setting precedents. But he is merciful and patient with people who sin due to weakness and who fail under pressure.

REGRETTED OUTBURSTS

People under the pressure of deep loss often say things they later regret. Let's look at a few Bible characters who did this and see what happened to them.

Thomas suffered deep loss when Christ was crucified. Not understanding the spiritual nature of the kingdom, he, along with the rest of the disciples, thought their dream of the past three years was shattered. Since the first day he had joined the band of thirteen, his hopes had been centered on Christ as deliverer of the oppressed Jews. Thomas surrendered other ambitions to follow this miracle worker.

In one horror-filled night, he lost it all. Jesus was dead, and Thomas didn't know whether his followers would be next or not. Thomas felt as if he had wasted years of his life on a foolish dream.

Three days later, the other disciples told him they'd seen Jesus alive. Were they playing some sort of practical joke? Was a look-alike trying to deceive them all?

"Unless I see the nail marks in his hands and put my finger where the nails were, and put my hand into his side, I will not believe it," he declared (John 20:25).

For his skepticism, he has earned the nickname "Doubting Thomas" and is often regarded with scorn. Yet when he *did* meet the resurrected Lord, Jesus discerned his heart attitude and gave him only the gentlest rebuke. Tradition tells us Thomas later took the gospel to India. Too bad he is remembered primarily for his moment of doubt.

A woman from Shunem showed hospitality to the gruff

What Does Our Map Say?

and outspoken prophet Elisha. To show his gratitude, Elisha told the barren woman she would have a son.

"Don't mislead me," she said, afraid to hope. The next year, she gave birth to a son.

Later, when the boy fell ill and died in her arms, her one thought was to get to Elisha. During the journey by donkey, she mulled everything around in her mind. When she finally reached the prophet, she let him have it.

" 'Did I ask you for a son, my lord?' she said. 'Didn't I tell you, "Don't raise my hopes"?' " (2 Kings 4:28).

This stern, no-nonsense prophet of God did not take offense at the blunt, almost accusatory statement. Elisha saw that the woman was in deep distress (v. 27), and he understood her outburst.

Elisha was never easily fooled. He had the God-given ability to discern heart attitudes. This was the same man who, two chapters earlier, had called down a curse on some youths jeering at his bald head. Two bears emerged from the woods and killed forty-two of the boys.

Heart attitude. It makes all the difference. "For he knows how we are formed, he remembers that we are dust" (Ps. 103:14). God understands when we fail under pressure. At the first sign of repentance, he forgives.

SO WHO PAYS?

The mercy and forgiveness of God are wonderful, but now we run into a slight theological problem. Because one of his attributes is holiness, God cannot overlook sin. Someone must pay the penalty. "The soul that sinneth, it shall die" (Ezek. 18:4 KJV).

No matter how much he might want to sweep our failures aside, he cannot, because a holy God cannot tolerate sin. Sin must be dealt with.

But our all-wise heavenly Father came up with a

solution. He paid the penalty himself by sending his sinless Son to die in our place and bear our sins. For us to benefit from this plan, however, we have to accept his substitutionary death.

When our heart attitude is rebellion, we do not value the blood of Jesus that washes us clean. God is patient, giving men and women every opportunity to repent. But if they continue to refuse his offer of free salvation from death, then they must pay the penalty themselves.

Christians sometimes feel that from the moment they become new creations in Christ, they must be perfect. No misstep is allowed. While perfection should certainly be our goal, we must realize that no one except Jesus is capable of living a sinless life.

The apostle John was addressing Christians when he wrote, "If we claim to be without sin, we deceive ourselves and the truth is not in us . . . . If we claim we have not sinned, we make him out to be a liar and his word has no place in our lives" (1 John 1:8,10).

Yet God does not hold a heavenly fly swatter over our heads to keep us in line. In between those two verses, John assures us, "If we confess our sins, he is faithful and just and will forgive us our sins and purify us from all unrighteousness" (1 John 1:9).

We need not suffer from guilt because of things we've said or done in the pain of loss. God has made a way to forgive us, and he is eager for us to accept it.

OKAY THEN, WHY *DO* WE LOSE?

Simply pointing out flaws in our basic assumptions is not enough to explain why we must experience loss—and anyone who has lost a treasure naturally seeks an answer. Of course, I don't know the reason in every situation, but I do believe we can discover some general reasons behind loss. Let's look at them in the next couple of chapters.

TIME TO CONSIDER

1. We generally hold one of three basic assumptions:
   • If we are righteous, God will bless and protect us.
   • If we suffer, it is because we have sinned.
   • If we sin, God will punish us.

Which belief do you identify with the most? Why?

2. In what ways might these beliefs help or hinder our relationship with God?

3. Find a scripture that promises or illustrates blessing in return for a righteous life, and one that promises or illustrates trials in spite of godly living. Do the verses seem contradictory? How might we reconcile them in our minds?

4. Have you ever been accused of suffering because of sin? Have you ever accused someone else? If so, how was it valid or invalid?

3

Those Hairpin Curves

Moving along life's trail, we inevitably encounter hairpin curves where we plunge into the canyon of loss. We may know that God did not push us off in punishment; but we wonder, *why must loss be part of the human experience?*

We do not have to look very far to see that loss is universal and comes to all people no matter where they live on the scale of risk-taking. Most of us drive on the freeway, build fires, fill a gas tank, take aspirin. Some people hardly ever leave home, wear safety belts when they do, eat organic vegetables, and never fly—yet loss comes to them, too.

Still others take "calculated risks." Mountain climbing, parachuting, living in a flood plain—where does one draw the line between foolhardiness and loss that is beyond human control? People tend to analyze each situation to determine who is at fault.

When a person blames himself, the loss can be viewed as a deserved punishment. Blaming others brings recriminations and the need to forgive. If fate is viewed as the culprit, one must believe that God does not ultimately control one's life. Blaming God can bring guilt and questions about God's trustworthiness.

For the Christian, most losses can be loosely grouped into three categories: loss by human action, loss by divine action, or loss as the result of divine inaction. Said differently, people throw something away, God takes it away, or God does not prevent its being taken away.

LOSS BY HUMAN ACTION

Some people lose because of their ignorance, revenge, misunderstandings, self-hate, or wrong motives. Some don't realize the value of their treasures, such as health or freedom, until they've thrown them away. Some willingly give up a treasure to get something they think is better. Peer pressure or "machismo" cause others to scorn safety precautions.

People who mourn loss due to their own actions often know who is to blame. Questions of "why?" usually arise as the result of misplaced faith or a misunderstanding of God's will as illustrated by a news story that, in the Fort Worth Press' opinion, "surpasses anything the imagination could conjure up."[1]

In 1973, Jim Fisher set sail in his thirty-one foot trimaran, the *Triton,* to do short-term missionary work in Costa Rica. His pregnant wife, Wilma, and their two small sons were to meet him in Costa Rica while Wilma's brother and sister-in-law, Bob and Linda Tininenko, went with him as crew.

Those Hairpin Curves

Four days into the journey, Bob and Linda discovered that Jim had set sail without his voice-transmission license because it had not arrived in time. Jim saw no problem with this. No danger would befall them out of God's will, anyway.

Nine days later, they encountered a severe storm off the California coast, and Jim was convinced that God had sent it as punishment for his deception. Throughout the night, Bob fought to keep the *Triton* from being sucked into one-hundred-foot-wide whirlpools while Jim thought about what he would do when it was his turn to take the helm. Should he interfere with God's will by challenging the storm?

If he called the Coast Guard for assistance, how would he explain his fraudulent use of the radio and his fictitious call letters? Not only would it mean risking the disgrace of conviction, the penalty could be two years in prison and a fine of ten thousand dollars.

Jim finally called the Coast Guard; but he told them, "Do not need assistance . . . . We are becalmed," even though Bob was still fighting to keep the *Triton* afloat in high winds and mountainous waves. After fourteen exhausting hours, Bob turned the helm over to Jim. Fifteen minutes later, a giant wave flipped the *Triton* upside down.

The three-hulled craft remained afloat upside down. As they salvaged what they could to prepare for survival, Bob noticed strange behavior in his brother-in-law. When a gallon of rice floated out of reach, Jim did not go after it. Days later, Bob discovered that Jim had thrown away some cheese and a big can of candy.

"We'll be rescued when God is ready for us to be rescued," Jim told him. "There's nothing we can do to bring on that moment. I don't see any need to start making plans and rationing food."

Who Says Winners Never Lose?

When Bob asked Jim for the water-distillation kit they had salvaged, Jim said he couldn't find it. "We must be totally dependent upon God," he said. "If we distilled water, then we would congratulate ourselves and perhaps live a long time and think that we did it all. I believe it is God's will that the kit is gone. We must be dependent upon the Lord."

Jim came to believe that God had brought the storm in order to bring Bob back to God. Bob resisted the idea. Not only was he bitter about their situation, he had left Jim's denomination a decade before over disagreement with church doctrine.

After they had capsized, Bob discovered that Linda was pregnant with their first child. Fighting morning sickness, she grew deathly ill on the skimpy rations. On the twenty-sixth day, she died.

Over the following weeks, the men survived on teaspoonfuls of food and swallows of water. On the seventy-third day lost at sea, they were rescued by a passing cargo ship at a point more than a thousand miles due west of Los Angeles. They had drifted almost halfway to Hawaii. Eleven days later, Jim died.

After physical therapy to restore his four-inch biceps and seven-inch thighs, Bob regained his physical health, but his spiritual health was seriously damaged. The last sentence in a book about his experience sums it up. "He would wrestle with God until the last day of his life."

The loss of two lives and the spiritual health of another occurred as a direct result of Jim's actions. That he sincerely believed he was doing right did not lessen the severity of the outcome.

In his zeal to not overstep God's will, Jim actually thwarted God's plan for their lives by *not* utilizing their resources for rescue. In at least four instances, Jim actively discarded God's providence.

1. *The safeguard of the law.* Sailing without his voice-transmission license made Jim reluctant to use the radio in time of need.

2. *Hesitance to ask for help.* Jim believed that acknowledging a need for rescue would be presumption before God, so he told the Coast Guard they did not need assistance. As a result, a search did not begin until the twelfth day of their ordeal.

At one point, a yellow coloration on the horizon convinced them they were close to Los Angeles. Hoping to capture some passing ship's attention, Bob piled oily rags on the hull while Jim napped. Bob trained a sun ray through a binocular lens onto the rags.

When Jim awoke and saw the black smoke, he began to weep. "You're interfering with God!" he cried. "This is not God's plan!" He wouldn't stop until Bob smothered the rags with salt water.

Eventually the search covered more than two hundred thousand square miles and was one of the Coast Guard's most massive searches in 1973. By this time, the shipwrecked crew had drifted many miles from shore, and the nearly flat hulls made them impossible to spot from the air.

3. *Discarding provisions.* Not only did Jim throw away food and the distillation kit, he at first refused to check the port outrigger for water bottles. "It won't do any good to look," he said. "I told you how I feel about interfering with the Lord's will."

4. *Discarding equipment.* When he thought he was dying, Jim confessed to cutting off the remainder of the mast and the sail underneath the trimaran on his first scuba dive—thus eliminating a way to steer themselves or increase their visibility. "I didn't think we should interfere with the Lord's will," he repeated.

Who Says Winners Never Lose?

Jim's fervent, fatalistic beliefs are not as unusual as one might suppose. In his book *Where Is God When It Hurts?*, Philip Yancey talks about other Christians who hold this view of God's will:

> Several years ago two researchers . . . studied victims of tornado damage across the country. They found that people in the South suffered a higher frequency of tornado-related deaths than Midwesterners, even after taking into account such factors as differences in building materials . . . . The researchers concluded that Southerners, being more religious, had developed a fatalistic attitude toward disaster: "If it hits, it hits, and there's nothing I can do to stop it." In contrast, Midwesterners listened to weather reports, secured loose equipment, and went to a safe place to wait out tornado warnings.
>
> "Alabamians were far more inclined than Illinoisans were to see their lives as controlled by external forces. The Southerners saw God as actively involved in their lives rather than as a benevolent but noninterfering presence.
>
> "Illinoisans tended to trust in technology to help them confront nature. But each Alabamian is on his own and faces the whirlwind alone with his God."
>
> If their conclusions are accurate, I take this as a dangerous perversion of Christian dogma . . . . Jesus Himself spent His life on earth fighting disease and despair. He never hinted at fatalism or a resigned acceptance of suffering. As members of a stained planet, we have the right, even the obligation, to battle the negative side-effects of man's fall.[2]

LOSS BY DIVINE ACTION

As we saw earlier, scripture states that God sometimes brings loss as punishment. But even when we think we know the situation, we should hesitate to label another's loss as a divine judgment.

A second kind of loss from divine action is the result of an "act of God"—"a sudden and irresistible action of natural forces, such as could not humanly have been foreseen or prevented." Such perils are beyond the scope of human containment.

Strange weather in 1988 caused catastrophes that affected millions of people. Four of these catastrophes had the distinction of setting records for disasters of their kind.

1. *The hottest summer.* The summer in 1988 was the driest and hottest since the 1930's Dust Bowl. The Mississippi River ran low, a heat wave closed Harvard University, and in Detroit, auto workers walked off the job when temperatures exceeded one hundred degrees.

Scorching heat and lack of rain withered crops and pasture land across the nation. This adversely impacted food prices and financially troubled family-owned farms.

2. *The worst forest fires.* Fires ravaged more than forty percent of Yellowstone National Park. Other fires in Washington, Idaho, Montana, Utah, Colorado, California, and Alaska brought the amount of charred land to nearly four million acres—an area larger than the state of Connecticut. The total far exceeded the areas blackened in 1985, the last "bad fire" year.

"An unusual combination of natural forces—hot weather, high winds, and an unrelenting summer drought—has been the primary culprit," said National Park Service Director William Mott.

3. *The worst floods.* In September, floods submerged

Who Says Winners Never Lose?

from seventy-five to ninety percent of Bangladesh. "I hate to sound hyperbolic," said Thomas Drahman, the Asia regional manager for CARE, "but this could be one of the largest natural disasters of the century."

4. *The worst hurricane.* Later in September, higher-than-normal ocean temperatures spawned Hurricane Gilbert, the most powerful storm to hit the western hemisphere in this century.

Wind destroyed four-fifths of Jamaica's houses, and damage to crops and tourist attractions virtually destroyed the island's economy. Tens of thousands were left homeless in Mexico. On the Gulf Coast, more than six inches of rain flooded an area the size of Colorado. At week's end, the storm had spun off some thirty tornadoes.

A reporter in *Time* magazine summed it up. "Somehow the storm seemed the violent culmination of a season in which Mother Nature has done anything but nurture, producing the hottest American summer in fifty years, a drought that parched the Midwest, forest fires that turned U.S. parks into cinders, floods that submerged large parts of Bangladesh and Sudan."[3]

Does being a Christian guarantee safety from meteorological dangers? Some people believe that it should. In times of peril, they take comfort in scriptures such as Psalm 91:3,10–12.

> Surely he will save you . . . no harm will befall you, no disaster will come near your tent. For he will command his angels concerning you to guard you in all your ways; they will lift you up in their hands, so that you will not strike your foot against a stone.

In spite of the psalmist's testimony of protection, we again must ask, does being a Christian *guarantee* safety

Those Hairpin Curves

from danger? What if that Christian has dedicated his or her life to serving God? One would think that full-time servants for the Lord could surely claim divine protection.

On June 9, 1972, one of the worst flood disasters in the nation began when fourteen to sixteen inches of rain poured into an area of South Dakota where normally only fourteen inches fall in an entire year.

Reverend Ron Masters, his wife LaVonne, and their five children watched the downpour from their parsonage in Rapid City. The telephone went dead, the lights flickered out, and water rose around the house.

When Ron and LaVonne lit candles and checked the basement, they discovered water pouring in through shattered window panes. They raced back upstairs, gathered the children, and waded to their four-wheel-drive Scout. They had barely crossed the bridge over Rapid Creek when a solid wall of water spun their vehicle downstream and jammed the bumper against a tree.

Water quickly filled the Scout. Ron, LaVonne, and their daughter Karen managed to get out, then two more walls of water hit them, nearly tearing them from the tree. During the long night, they were surrounded by chaos—torrential rains, lightning, falling trees, fire-spitting gas tanks, hurling debris, screaming victims, and homes and dead bodies sweeping past. They prayed desperately.

In the morning, the water receded and they saw the Scout still lodged against a tree. Their youngest daughter had survived the night in an air pocket but their two oldest sons had suffocated in the vehicle. Two-and-a-half weeks later, a rescue worker discovered the body of their toddler lodged in a tree downstream.

Was God merely a spectator while Nature unleashed that freak storm? Scripture plainly states that God takes responsibility for the weather. "He causes his sun to rise on the

Who Says Winners Never Lose?

evil and the good, and sends rain on the righteous and the unrighteous" (Matt. 5:45). "I form the light and create darkness, I bring prosperity and create disaster; I, the Lord, do all these things" (Isa. 45:7).

Hurricane Gilbert tore roofs off shacks, mansions, brothels, churches, hospitals, and resorts. Neither the purpose of the building nor the spiritual condition of the owner made any difference in how much a building was damaged. Clearly, disasters affect everyone—the righteous and the unrighteous alike.

LOSS BY DIVINE INACTION

Regardless of the cause, we ask, "Why didn't God prevent the loss?"

When a killer tornado ripped through Albion, Pennsylvania, the Stahlsmith family sought refuge in their cellar. As the twister demolished the house around them, a cellar wall collapsed and killed six-year-old Luke while his mother tried to shelter him in her arms.

"If it had just been a tornado wrecking our house, that would be easy to get over," Sandra Stahlsmith said later. "Material things can be replaced. But with Luke, I don't ever expect to get over it.... You wonder where your angels were who were supposed to be watching over you."

Philip Yancey ponders the question.

Does our God reach down, slightly twist the wheels of school buses, and watch them carom through guardrails? Does He draw a red pencil line through a map of Indiana to plan the exact path a tornado should take? *There, hit that house, kill that six-year-old, but hop up and skip this next house.* Does God jostle the earth, playing with tidal waves, earthquake tremors, and hurricanes ... squashing men out like cigarette butts?

Those Hairpin Curves

Is that how He rewards and punishes us, His helpless victims?

Posing the questions may sound sacrilegious. But they've haunted me and other Christians I know. And they've been tossed at me like spears by scoffing friends....

If God is truly in charge, somehow connected to all the world's suffering, why is He so capricious, unfair?

How does God fit into this world He has made for us? Does He hover close above us, reaching in now and then to break an arm, cause a tragic death, unleash a flood? Or does He silently let the world slump along with its wars, tragedies, and violent history.[4]

What about the guardrails that are supposed to keep us from falling into the abyss of loss? Does a God of love ever pull them out at the very moment we round a dangerous curve? For those who have suffered loss, these questions are more than just topics for a seminary debate team. The answers may determine whether or not a person feels he or she can continue to trust in God.

TIME TO CONSIDER

1. Losses can generally be grouped into three categories:
   - loss by human action
   - loss by divine action
   - loss by divine inaction

Which have you experienced most? How did you respond?

2. Is one type of loss more devastating than another? Why or why not?

Who Says Winners Never Lose?

3. How does loss by human action influence beliefs toward mankind? How does loss by divine action or inaction influence beliefs toward God?

4. Have you successfully worked through a loss in your life? What steps did you take to overcome the loss?

5. Do you seem unable to accept a loss? What beliefs, feelings, or actions might be hindering acceptance?

4

What About the Guardrails?

God does not want puppets for subjects. He knew all along that Adam and Eve would choose the prospect of enlightenment over obedience; but in spite of that, he still gave humanity a free will.

Mankind has been choosing sin ever since. Lying, looting, loss of the ozone layer—all result from mankind's greedy choices. We must remember that, in allowing man his freedom of choice, God does not overrule the consequences of those choices. The guardrails will not hold us if we choose to smash through them.

Some feel that this "permission of God" explains why we must experience loss. We lose because we live on a fallen, imperfect planet that is nothing at all like God's original design. All of us suffer the consequences of our own and others' bad choices, and we will not experience

Who Says Winners Never Lose?

emancipation until we reach heaven. According to this view, God does not cause loss; he simply cannot prevent it without overriding our freedom of choice.

In developing this belief as it relates to pain and suffering, Philip Yancey studied God's dealings with people in the Bible. Looking at the bloody history, the warnings of the prophets, and the reward/punishment concept in the Psalms, he noticed that God rarely intervened with miracles in Old Testament times.

When Jesus took on the form of man and entered human history, he used miracles as illustrations of deeper truths. Yet sometimes he did not intervene in the natural order of things. To the question, "Who is responsible for suffering?" Jesus gave mixed answers (Luke 13:1,2,4,16; John 9:1–3).

Philip Yancey concluded with these thoughts.

> Because of biblical hints like these, I doubt the view that God directly causes suffering to teach us specific lessons . . . .
>
> I have been with sick Christian people who torment themselves with the question, "What is God trying to teach me?"
>
> . . . Maybe they have it all wrong. Maybe God *isn't trying to tell us anything specific* each time we hurt. Pain and suffering are part and parcel of our planet, and Christians are not exempt. Half the time we know why we get sick: too little exercise, a poor diet, contact with a germ. Do we really expect God to go around protecting us whenever we encounter something dangerous?[1]

When Satan Brings Loss

Scripture clearly teaches that loss is sometimes caused

What About the Guardrails?

by Satan. "Your enemy the devil prowls around like a roaring lion looking for someone to devour" (1 Pet. 5:8).

I do not include loss by Satan's action as one of the major categories because believers do not live at the mercy of the devil. While those unprotected by the blood of Jesus *do* suffer great loss at the enemy's hand, God has given Christians power over him. God may give Satan permission to touch us for a season, as he did Job; but such instances are always monitored and limited by God.

We read in scripture of times that Satan brought loss. Besides Job, a crippled woman had been bound by Satan for eighteen years. In the parable of the four soils, Satan snatched the word from people who heard it. Paul said he wanted to visit the church at Thessalonica "but Satan stopped us" (1 Thess. 2:18).

We are to be constantly on the alert against Satan's devices. When Paul counseled the church at Corinth, he explained that he did what he did "that Satan might not outwit us. For we are not unaware of his schemes" (2 Cor. 2:11). Paul told Timothy that a pastor is to maintain a good reputation with outsiders "so that he will not fall into disgrace and into the devil's trap" (1 Tim. 3:7).

Many times, God intervenes by sending a guardian angel to protect us as he did when Daniel was thrown to the lions and when an angel warned Joseph to flee with Mary and baby Jesus to Egypt.

At other times, we are to come against Satan ourselves. Jesus set the example when he was tempted. "Away from me, Satan!" he commanded (Matt. 4:10). The apostle Paul urges us to clothe ourselves fully in God's armor, "so that you can take your stand against the devil's schemes" (Eph. 6:11). James exhorts us to "resist the devil, and he will flee from you" (James 4:7).

While Christians have the authority to resist Satan,

Who Says Winners Never Lose?

unbelievers do not. Jude tells of ungodly men who, among other things, slandered celestial beings. To show the danger they were in, Jude said "Even the archangel Michael, when he was disputing with the devil about the body of Moses, did not dare to bring a slanderous accusation against him, but said, 'The Lord rebuke you!'" (Jude 9).

When Satan comes against believers, we are to resist his attacks. Jesus told his followers, "I have given you authority . . . to overcome all the power of the enemy; nothing will harm you" (Luke 10:19).

Is God Able?

When loss comes in spite of all we've done to prevent it, some people feel the issue goes far deeper than God choosing not to interfere. "Either God has the love to remove human misery but doesn't have the power," they reason, "or he has the power but not the love. It's even possible he has neither, but he certainly doesn't have both."

In his best-selling book, *When Bad Things Happen to Good People*, Rabbi Harold Kushner interprets the book of Job as saying that God wants good people to live peaceful, happy lives, but he doesn't always have the power to bring it about. "It is too difficult even for God to keep cruelty and chaos from claiming their innocent victims."[2]

We know this cannot be true because one of God's attributes is omnipotence—he is all-powerful. The prophet Jeremiah declared, "Ah, Sovereign Lord . . . . Nothing is too hard for you" (Jer. 32:17). Jesus himself said, "With God all things are possible" (Matt. 19:26).

THE PROVIDENCE OF GOD

A different view from Rabbi Kushner's and those who believe in the "permission of God" is that, after creation, God did not abandon us to swirl through the universe at the

What About the Guardrails?

mercy of the elements and our bad choices. He is directly concerned with every minute of our lives and allows nothing to befall us that is not in his will.

The apostle Paul said of Christ, "For by him all things were created . . . and in him all things hold together" (Col. 1:16,17). Not only did he create the universe, he continually maintains it. This includes the stars (Isa. 40:26), food and water for nature (Ps. 147:8,9), our life and movement (Acts 17:28), and seed for planting and daily food (2 Cor. 9:10).

In his book, *Trusting God Even When Life Hurts*, Jerry Bridges discusses the control God has over our lives.

> Every breath we breathe is a gift from God, every bite of food we eat is given to us from His hand, every day we live is determined by Him. He has not left us to our own devices, or the whims of nature, or the malevolent acts of other people . . . .
>
> The . . . problem with our popular use of the expression "the providence of God" is that we either unconsciously or deliberately imply that God intervenes at specific points in our lives but is largely only an interested spectator most of the time. When we think this way, even unconsciously, we reduce God's control over our lives to a stop-and-go, in-and-out proposition. Our unconscious attitude is that the rest of the time we are the "master of our fates" or conversely the victims of unhappy circumstances or uncaring people that cross our paths.
>
> *God's providence is His constant care for and His absolute rule over all His creation for His own glory and the good of His people* . . . . Nothing, not even the smallest virus, escapes His care and control.[3]

Who Says Winners Never Lose?

God's Love for Us

When we are convinced that God has the power to prevent loss, but we lose anyway, we may wonder if God really loves us. How could a loving God allow us to suffer so deeply or for so long? The Bible says God is love. How can we receive assurance of it?

The sacrifice of Jesus should convince us. One reason we partake of communion is so we will remember the greatest love gift of all. God sent his only Son to bear our sins and pay sin's penalty with his death. Did he do it because he was merely fond of us? Of course not. An overwhelming love caused him to sacrifice his Son on our behalf. He couldn't stand to be separated from us, even while we were sinners.

Such love isn't going to diminish after we are reconciled with God. As Paul wrote to the Romans, "He who did not spare his own Son, but gave him up for us all—how will he not also, along with him, graciously give us all things?" (Rom. 8:32).

Scripture also tells us that God's love can never fail (Isa. 54:10; Ps. 13:5). In our losses, Satan will whisper that God has forsaken us, that a God of love would not treat us so badly. At such times, we must accept by faith what we do not feel in our emotions. "The Bible says God always loves me. I choose to believe it."

Opposing Views?

We've looked at God's permission and God's providence. What can we conclude from these seemingly opposing views? Although we must suffer the consequences of our choices in this fallen world, God has the power to sustain us every moment of our lives. Even when Satan attacks us, God has given us power to overcome. This means that when we experience loss, it never occurs outside God's love and plan for our lives.

Why Does God Allow Loss?

If God controls the smallest details of our lives and if he loves us as Scripture says, what possible reasons can he have for allowing us to suffer loss?

We will look at five reasons and cover the last three in more depth in a later chapter on turning loss into gain.

1. *Loss reveals our need for God.* Pride, the first sin, caused Lucifer's fall from heaven. We have suffered from pride ever since. If we had no problems, we'd be apt to think we could handle affairs on our own. Loss causes us to see God at work in our lives.

As author and editor Bert Ghezzi puts it, "If we had no difficulties, we might go about our lives imagining we have everything under control, like little gods who see no need for God. The Lord mercifully lets us have problems that make us face reality. When we finally turn to Him, we will agree the pain was worth it."[4]

2. *Loss tests us.* When the Israelites finally entered the promised land after their forty-year trek around the Negev, they did not immediately pitch tents wherever they liked. They had to first destroy the people who lived there. That's what the famous battle of Jericho was all about. God defeated Jericho for his people. He defeated other fortified cities, too, in wonderful, supernatural ways. But eventually God tired of the Israelite's disobedience and told them:

> "Because this nation has violated the covenant that I laid down for their forefathers and has not listened to me, I will no longer drive out before them any of the nations Joshua left when he died. I will use them to test Israel and see whether they will keep the way of the Lord and walk in it as their forefathers did."

Who Says Winners Never Lose?

> They were left to test the Israelites to see whether they would obey the Lord's commands, which he had given their forefathers through Moses (Judg. 2:20–22; 3:4).

One does not prove loyalty to a king by eating delicacies in a warm banquet hall. Knighthood is earned by slaying dragons and rescuing princesses at extreme danger to one's own life and limb. Loss tests our loyalty to the King of kings.

Satan contended that Job served God merely because God blessed and protected him. "Why shouldn't he, when you pay him so well?" Satan scoffed. God allowed Job's trial for the purpose of proving Satan wrong.

When we encounter difficulties, our reaction shows God—and everyone else who is watching—the true depth of our loyalty to him.

3. *Loss teaches us.* God left unconquered nations in the promised land for another reason—"to teach warfare to the descendants of the Israelites who had not had previous battle experience" (Judg. 3:2).

One might wonder why God did not simply see to it that the men never again had to fight. He could have banished enemies forever and instituted permanent peace. Instead, he wanted the inexperienced to become experienced, and what better way to learn than by doing?

The boot camp of loss teaches Christians how to fight in spiritual warfare. From loss, we learn how to handle future losses, how to view life in its proper perspective, and we learn valuable skills for comforting others.

    a. *Loss teaches us how to handle future losses.* Recovering from small losses gives us skills to handle large ones. Sometimes it works the other way around. After losing my son, I found that small losses did not affect me the way

What About the Guardrails?

they used to. After all, how can spoiled food in a warm refrigerator compare with the death of one's baby?

I used to worry about having enough money to live on. When we went through lean times early in our marriage and I saw God's provision again and again, I learned we could trust him for our daily needs. God had brought us through large losses; smaller losses would not defeat us.

b. *Loss teaches us perspective*. The Koshak family thought they lived far enough away from the beach that they and their friends could ride out the fury of hurricane Camille in 1969. When the raging sea blasted the front door open and began to flood the house, it was too late to flee to higher ground.

The fifteen children and adults huddled on the stairs, which were protected by two interior walls. As the water rose up the steps, the first-floor exterior walls collapsed. They ran to an inside room on the second floor.

A moment later, the wind lifted off the roof, exposing them to slashing rain. Second-story walls disintegrated around them. The group huddled under a mattress against a remaining wall and watched water lap toward them across the slanting floor. Just when hope failed, the wind diminished slightly and the water stopped rising.

After it was over, Grandmother Koshak reflected: "We lost practically all our possessions, but the family came through it. When I think of that, I realize we lost nothing important."

c. *Loss teaches us skills to comfort others*. No one understands losing everything by fire, as well as people who have been burned out themselves. Those who lose loved ones quickly learn what comforts others in bereavement. But they did not possess those skills until they learned from their own losses.

Paul called God "the God of all comfort, who comforts

Who Says Winners Never Lose?

us in all our troubles, so that we can comfort those in any trouble with the comfort we ourselves have received from God" (2 Cor. 1:3,4).

4. *Loss enables us to gain.* Mary lost her reputation, her comfort, and she nearly lost her fiancé in order to gain the privilege of becoming the Messiah's mother.

Jochebed lost the presence of her baby, Moses, while he slept in the bulrushes. She was denied contact with him while he grew up in the palace as the adopted son of the Egyptian princess. She didn't see him for forty years after he killed a man and hid in the wilderness. But all her losses led directly to the gain of seeing her son become the Hebrew slaves' emancipator.

Ruth lost a husband, her income, and even her homeland. As a result, she gained a wealthy husband, the honor of her adopted countrymen, and she became an ancestor of Christ.

Some gains are not possible without a prior loss. Often God allows us to lose in order that we may receive a tremendous blessing.

5. *Loss produces godliness.* As someone once said, "God cares more about our character than our comfort." Loss is a full-time teacher in God's character improvement course, and every man or woman who wants to be used of God must enroll.

If Jesus "learned obedience from what he suffered" and in so doing was "made perfect" (Heb. 5:8,9), how much more do we grow spiritually in difficult times? God's primary work is not to shield us from suffering, but to conform us to the image of his son (Rom. 8:29 KJV).

God uses torment, pain, sorrow, failure, and loss to produce men and women who stir their generations for God. Study the lives of the great leaders in the Bible, both men and women, and you will find each one suffered loss. Before he calls us into service, God builds character.

What About the Guardrails?

Trusting God in the Tunnel

Sometimes, rather than plunging us over the cliff, loss thrusts us deep into a tunnel where we can't see God, hear his voice, or feel his leading.

Back on the sunlit path, we may have been convinced of his love and leading; now when we need him most desperately, he is silent—or may even seem to contradict what he has said before.

Engulfed in the thick darkness and feeling totally alone, we may think we cannot endure the losses that God demands we survive. We look for a purpose, but our losses defy categorization. Where is the God of love who said he would never leave us nor forsake us?

We need to remember—in the tunnel—that we cannot trust our senses. Strange subterranean noises will echo around us, whipping up panic, and confusing our sense of direction. The devil's whispers of discouragement will come alive in our imaginations.

At all costs, tunnel travelers must keep going. Those who give up in despair will remain trapped in the darkness. God's love always shines on us, and God is always thinking thoughts of peace toward us (Jer. 29:11 KJV), even when the tunnel wall temporarily obscures them.

Our future does not and never did depend on what we lost. Our future does not depend on our spouse, how much money we have, our health, or our social position. Our future only and always depends on God. Not only does he work around losses, he bestows beauty instead of ashes (Isa. 61:3).

God has not promised we would never suffer loss. He didn't promise we wouldn't have questions, grief, or difficulties in our lives. But he has promised he will not abandon us. He cares for us and loves us and will continue to lead us.

Who Says Winners Never Lose?

Remember that God not only created us, he chose the family and country into which we were born. While taking into consideration our freedom of choice, he planned our lives down to the last detail, including the seemingly random gains and losses of life. As Jerry Bridges puts it, "All these situations and circumstances, though they may appear only as happenstance to us, were written in God's book before one of them came to be."[5]

This all-wise Planner of ours is not obligated to explain his reasons to us. He is sovereign. He is good. We can trust him.

He may be silent when we lose a treasure. In the tunnel, we may not see any purpose for the loss. But no matter what the limits of our sight or emotions may be, *we can always trust God. Even when we lose.*

TIME TO CONSIDER

1. With which of the two views of God's interaction with our loss do you identify, God's permission or God's providence? How has your view helped or hindered you as you work through loss?

2. Loss teaches us how to handle future losses, how to gain perspective on loss, and how to allow loss to produce gain in our lives. Which of these have you experienced? How?

3. In the black tunnel of loss, it's easy to despair. Which unshakable qualities of God can we depend on as we travel through the tunnel? How can we hang on to these qualities when our loss and pain seem to contradict them?

Part II
The Treasures We Lose

5

Loss of Possessions

The losses that Job and his wife experienced cover the spectrum of loss in our lives today. Nearly everything we lose fits into one of the following categories:
- loss of possessions
- loss of loved ones
- loss of health
- loss of dignity and other intangibles
- loss of faith in God

No matter what the deprivation, we will experience some degree of grief because we react to the loss of anything or anyone we have given to and received from.

Job's first loss was that of possessions. In his day, when wealth was counted in livestock, Job was very rich. He had seven thousand sheep, three thousand camels, five hundred oxen, five hundred donkeys, and many servants.

Who Says Winners Never Lose?

One day, the Sabeans carried off the oxen and donkeys, fire from the sky burned up the sheep, and Chaldeans carried off the camels. At each disaster scene, all the servants were killed except for one who escaped to report the catastrophe to Job. In a few hours, Job fell from his position as the richest man in the East to complete poverty.

Possessions can be classified into three groups—those necessary for our well-being such as food, shelter, clothing, and medical care; possessions that are not necessary for our survival but whose loss can change the way we live; and luxuries we don't need but which give us enjoyment. Loss from any of these categories can cause grief.

Yet when someone loses a possession, people are not usually sympathetic. When furniture is repossessed, they say, "It wasn't really yours anyway." People who've lost everything in a fire hear, "Just be thankful your family got out alive."

While we can be grateful for what remains, such commendable attitudes do not replace the loss. Nothing will. Loss must be realized and grieved before healing can come.

In March, 1986, our friend Kathy came home to find three fire trucks in her yard and all the upstairs windows blown out from intense heat. When she later accompanied the fire chief upstairs to view the damage, they discovered everything melted together—toys, clothes, beds. Kathy noticed the charred and melted remains of many books, tapes, and records from the public library and thought fleetingly of how much she would be charged for their loss. Covering it all was a foot of loose insulation that had sifted through the burned places in the ceiling.

When the four children followed her in, one of them picked up a burnt toy. "Oh, my Cabbage Patch doll! Oh, my Cabbage Patch doll!" she mourned.

"The only way I got through the first night was by

Loss of Possessions

reading all the scriptures I'd ever underlined," Kathy told me. "By morning I had peace."

The children stayed with friends for several days but later regretted the decision. One girl had nightmares until she was back home. After the worst of the mess was cleaned up, the children slept on the floor downstairs for two months.

The second blow came when the family discovered that through some clerical oversight, they were not covered by fire insurance. Although this family lost "only possessions," it profoundly affected their way of life and brought them much grief.

Sometimes we hesitate to mention our lost treasure for fear people will not understand our feelings over losing "only things." Ira Tanner comments:

> When we tell someone we "feel bad" at the death of a houseplant that has hung in our kitchen for five years, we cannot predict their response. Fond themselves of houseplants and believing their care is not a waste of time or money, they will empathize with our feelings; devoid of interest in plants, their reaction to our loss may be one of bewilderment.[1]

I vividly remember the last day of first grade when the teacher told us to clean out our desks and save a few of our best papers to take home.

I couldn't tell time yet and did not know how long she was giving us to complete the task. My desk was stuffed with graded tests I wanted to show my parents. I'd also prepared many drawings for my California grandparents who were due to visit that summer.

Carefully, I smoothed a sketch of Mickey Mouse I was especially proud of and placed it beside a spelling paper

Who Says Winners Never Lose?

with one hundred percent at the top. Would I have time to go through all my papers before the bell rang? I seemed to have more than the other children. How awful if we were dismissed while my desk was still a mess.

Stacking everything as neatly as I could, I sat for a long time, keeping a watchful eye on the clock in case it should suddenly begin to make sense. Surely the bell would ring at any moment, and since I had waited so long, I didn't dare start going through the papers now.

When the bell rang, we lined up at the door. The teacher's hawk-like gaze scanned the row and settled on me. "You can't take all that home," she barked. She scooped up my treasures, and I never saw them again.

No one else would consider that stack of scribbles to have any value. But I did. I felt a great loss and resented my teacher for many years.

We experience loss even on the happy occasion of buying something new. Ira Tanner uses the family car as an example.

> Each day we grieve the loss of *something, someone,* or *some place* important to us. Here is Jim, for instance, who has bought a new car. He likes all of its fancy new features, among them an FM radio and electric windows, but he also grieves the loss of the old car, an eight-year-old model. The family took it on several memorable vacations and, as with anything that serves us well, they grew to trust its dependability and became attached to it. We grieve the loss of any object in which we have invested not only our money but our time and affection as well. Jim and his family "loved" that old car and it is perfectly normal that they grieve its loss.[2]

Loss of Possessions

In scripture, we see people who lost possessions and grieved over them. For instance, Esau didn't seem to think much of his birthright when it was still an intangible, far-off promise. Famished from hunting, he traded it for a bowl of his brother's lentil stew. When the large inheritance of his father's estate became actual possessions, Esau "sought it carefully with tears" but it was too late (Heb. 12:17 KJV).

When some Old Testament prophets were chopping down a tree to construct a new building, an iron ax head flew off the handle and sank in a nearby body of water. This loss was worsened by the fact that the ax was borrowed.

Rather than scorn the loss as too trivial to waste God's power on, Elisha performed a miracle and the ax head floated to the surface for recovery (2 Kings 6:1–7).

As Jesus was on his way to raise Jairus' daughter, "a woman was there who had been subject to bleeding for twelve years. She had suffered a great deal under the care of many doctors and had spent all she had, yet instead of getting better she grew worse" (Mark 5:25,26).

Tucked into the dramatic story of how this woman received healing by merely touching the hem of Jesus' robe is the reference to her having "spent all she had." Not only had her condition grown worse while she suffered the humiliation of being unclean according to Jewish law, she had lost all her money.

This material loss was a bitter side effect of her futile search for healing.

POSSESSIONS AS SERVANTS

Possessions perform tasks for us, save us time, and make our lives easier. Because we are accustomed to their faithful service, their loss can affect our lifestyle and cause us grief.

When Corrie ten Boom was arrested for hiding Jews in

her home, she was unable to take with her a small bag of necessities she had prepared for just such an occasion.

Now in solitary confinement, suffering from a raging fever, and with rotting straw to lie on and a vomit-soaked blanket for warmth, she mourned the bag's loss.

> That prison bag ... how many times I opened it in my mind and pawed through all the things I had left behind. A fresh blouse. Aspirin, a whole bottle of them. Toothpaste with a kind of pepperminty taste, and—
>
> Then I would catch myself. How ridiculous, such thoughts! If I had it to do again would I really put these little personal comforts ahead of human lives? Of course not. But in the dark nights, as the wind howled and the fever pulsed, I would draw that bag out of some dark corner of my mind and root through it once again. A towel to lay on this scratchy straw. An aspirin.... [3]

When Corrie finally received a package from a friend, its simple contents of a sweater, cookies, vitamins, needle and thread, and a red towel brightened her bleak existence and were like treasures from heaven.

POSSESSIONS AS GODS

The Prosperity Movement teaches that if we give our tithes and offerings to the work of the church, the Lord will prosper us beyond our imagination. Tony Campolo remarks, "Such claims are made in spite of the fact that there are tens of thousands of people in Third World nations who love the Lord, obey His Law, faithfully tithe, and yet suffer privation beyond our comprehension."[4]

Wealth and the possessions it buys can delude us into self-sufficiency and make us think we don't need God.

Loss of Possessions

When possessions become our gods, we find it easy to protect our own economic interests rather than being concerned about others who lack.

When someone in the crowd asked Jesus, "Teacher, tell my brother to divide the inheritance with me," Jesus replied, "Watch out! Be on your guard against all kinds of greed; a man's life does not consist in the abundance of his possessions" (Luke 12:13,15).

Paul warned Timothy, "For the love of money is a root of all kinds of evil. Some people, eager for money, have wandered from the faith and pierced themselves with many griefs" (1 Tim. 6:10).

If possessions become gods to us, and the Lord takes them away to draw us back to him, we will know it. We will not need friends to point it out.

When we are tempted to be like Job's friends, let's remember that we cannot be certain of what God is doing in someone else's life. The Lord became angry at Eliphaz, Bildad, and Zophar because they assumed Job had sinned. Let's be careful not to add to the grief a person feels when suffering the loss of a possession.

Kathy is still amazed at the wonderful way people pitched in to help after the fire. Men from the church came the next day and began shoveling out the charred rubble. Relatives washed every square inch of the downstairs, including all the dishes in the kitchen cupboards. People from all over brought groceries, clothes, and toys.

The church took an offering of more than two thousand dollars for them, and the women's group collected money to buy new clothes for Kathy. One lady sewed Cabbage Patch-type dolls for the children, and another bought one from the store.

"After the first two or three days, it was not traumatic for me," Kathy remembers. "Everyone was so kind; I felt loved

Who Says Winners Never Lose?

and supported. After the first shock, it was blessing after blessing because of all that people were bringing. I'd gone to church all my life and had never seen the church pull together like that. They were united in one purpose."

Loss of possessions causes grief. Let us remember to be sensitive to people suffering this loss and allow God's love to flow through us as we minister to them.

TIME TO CONSIDER

1. Job and his wife experienced loss in five areas:
   - possessions
   - loved ones
   - health
   - dignity and other intangibles
   - faith in God

In which areas have you experienced loss?

2. If you have lost possessions, did you experience grief? If yes, did it surprise you? Why or why not?

3. At what point do possessions cross the line from being servants to being gods? What perspective or steps might help us reduce an over-dependence on possessions?

6

Loss of Loved Ones

Job's ten children were at the oldest brother's home for dinner when a whirlwind shrieked out of the desert and demolished the house, killing them all.

The one surviving servant who fled to report it arrived at the very moment Job learned he had become a pauper.

Perhaps Job's deepest loss was the death of his children. Remember, those sons and daughters belonged to his wife, too. She went through unanesthetized labor with each one and breast-fed them through infancy. Together, Job and his wife nurtured them through childhood and young adulthood. Now they were both childless.

One book written to help pastors comfort others in grief defines the death of a loved one as:

... The shattering of a significant relationship, a feeling of emptiness inside, a collapse of plans, a shriveling of hope, and sometimes a radical restructuring of life when there is no strength or desire to undertake the task. In some cases, of course, death comes as a relief; in many cases, however, it is an unmitigated horror.... But in every case, if one accepts the Biblical view, death is a horrendous abnormality, a grotesque perversion of a God-created order, a violent ripping of what ought to be a seamless fabric.[1]

When our son died, I felt as if part of my heart had been torn out, roots and all, leaving a bloody, throbbing hole in my inner being. A long time passed before I found a reason to smile, laugh, or sing. For many months, I was convinced I would never again be happy on this earth.

Losing a loved one produces severe emotional pain, to say nothing of physical reactions. The bereaved person may become agitated, hysterical, bitter, withdrawn, bewildered, or apathetic; the loss may trigger mild sadness, prolonged melancholia, or even suicidal despair.

LOSS OF A CHILD

"The death of a child is said to be the most devastating death. It is the one we least expect, the one we deny and fear the most," writes Joan Bordow in *The Ultimate Loss: Coping with the Death of a Child.*[2]

No matter the age of the child, whether infant, adult, or in between, parents are devastated when their children die. According to grief expert Dr. Nancy O'Conner, "The role of parent is to live, protect, teach and nurture your child. Parents *expect* to die before their children. It is the natural order of life events. When the situation is

Loss of Loved Ones

reversed and a child dies before the parents it seems wrong."[3]

When Herod attempted to get rid of Jesus by commanding that all the boys in Bethlehem two years old or younger be killed, the bereaved mothers mourned so deeply, they refused to be comforted (Matt. 2:16–18). In fact, the prophet Jeremiah had foretold of this tragedy by emphasizing the mothers' grief (see Jeremiah 31:15).

Even though Absalom had tried to steal the throne from his father David, the king was deeply shaken when the young man was killed. At the news, he wept, "O my son Absalom! My son, my son Absalom! If only I had died instead of you—O Absalom, my son, my son!" (2 Sam. 18:33).

THE LOSS OF A SPOUSE

Many widowed people feel incomplete without their "other half." The shared dreams, the emotional closeness, and the years of growth together are now mere memories. A young widow or widower may feel cheated that they cannot share children, fun times, and goals with the deceased spouse.

, Even people who had problems in the marriage will miss the other person's presence. The opportunity to solve those problems is gone.

We read in the Old Testament of a prophet who died, leaving a wife and two boys. The body was hardly cold when the dead man's creditor demanded the two boys as his slaves in payment for a debt. The widow not only faced emotional grief and the shock of her husband's death, she now faced the imminent loss of her sons as well. Elisha performed a miracle so that she could pay the debt and keep her little family together (see 2 Kings 4:1–7).

While it's not customary to send sympathy cards at the

loss of a spouse through divorce, the loss is traumatic nonetheless. One pastor points out, "It is almost like a living death to see the one whom you continue to love turning his back on you, figuratively slapping you in the face."[4]

Even less recognized is the loss felt at the death of a divorced spouse. People do grieve the happy times they had together, and guilt often compounds these feelings.

THE LOSS OF PARENTS

The age of the child influences how well he or she will handle losing a parent. When the child is young, the grief may remain unresolved for years. This can also happen in later years when the death is sudden or the relationship tense.

My father died of leukemia when I was twenty-one and just getting to know him as an adult. The loss I mourned most was the growing camaraderie, sharing with him what I was learning in college, and the resulting animated discussions. I lost not only a father, but a friend.

Scripture says that when Isaac married Rebekah, he "brought her into the tent of his mother Sarah . . . and he loved her; and Isaac was comforted after his mother's death" (Gen. 24:67).

Even though Sarah was quite elderly—she had been ninety years old when Isaac was born—her death was still a loss to him.

THE LOSS OF SIBLINGS

On the day of our son's funeral, our family doctor called to see how we were doing. "You should probably have a talk with Aimee," he said. "Children often think they are responsible when someone dies."

In numbness, I thanked him. Privately, I doubted our

Loss of Loved Ones

almost-four-year-old would take responsibility. We had been so open with her about his cancer, and she had often been at his side when he received treatments.

Just in case, I asked if she knew why he had died. She nodded. "It's because I pushed him one day when we were playing, and he hit his head."

Startled, I gathered her in my arms and again told her what had really happened. For many months afterward, she continued to ask me, "Why did Brother die?" I explained in a variety of ways until her preoccupation with the subject faded.

When adult siblings die, a deep feeling of sorrow occurs, like losing some part of oneself. Separation or distance lessen the impact of the death. Unresolved conflicts may bring guilt or regret.

LOSSES OTHERS MAY NOT UNDERSTAND

1. *The loss of friends*. Although most people understand the grief at a family member's death, fewer people realize the trauma one goes through when a friend dies.

Not only do we miss the person's companionship, we are reminded of our own mortality. If the friend has been part of our regular schedule—coffee klatches, fishing trips, frequent phone calls, a coworker—we will have daily reminders of our loss.

Before Winnie became our church organist, she played the piano while Brother Henry played the organ. Though blind, he wasn't bitter about his condition and sought to serve God any way he could.

Winnie appreciated his sweet spirit and inspiration to the entire church. She felt they were a well-tuned team during times of worship. He relied on her to communicate such things as key changes and the order of service.

When Brother Henry passed away, his granddaughter

Who Says Winners Never Lose?

asked Winnie to be the organist at his funeral. "I don't know if I can make it through the service," Winnie said, but she went.

At church, someone noticed she had been crying. "You look terrible!" the woman said. "You act like he was your own father or something."

The remark upset Winnie. "I probably miss him more than anyone else other than family," she retorted.

Even though King Saul sought to kill David, Saul's son Jonathan was David's best friend for years. When David learned of Jonathan's death, he wrote a lament. "I grieve for you, Jonathan my brother; you were very dear to me. Your love for me was wonderful, more wonderful than that of women" (2 Sam. 1:26).

2. *The loss of others.* The death of more distant relatives will be hard on us if we have enjoyed a close relationship with them. Grandparents, favorite aunts or uncles, cousins, stepsiblings, stepparents, foster families—the closeness of our relationship determines our degree of grief when we lose them.

We are also affected by the deaths of ministers, mentors, counselors, role models, former teachers, and baby-sitters. Even if we have not been in contact with them for years, we may feel deep sadness and loss because they had a part in our development.

When Dorcas died, the weeping widows who showed Peter the clothing she had made them were not saddened just because their source of apparel was gone. They genuinely loved her and keenly sensed their loss. When Peter raised her from the dead and presented her to the believers and widows, "this became known all over Joppa, and many people believed in the Lord" (Acts 9:42).

We feel loss at the death of people we don't know personally. When John F. Kennedy, Pope John XXIII, and the

Loss of Loved Ones

Challenger astronauts died, people of every nationality mourned. The world seems poorer when our heroes die.

My husband experienced loss when Louis L'Amour died, not only because his favorite author would no longer provide him with additional reading enjoyment, but he admired this man who could spin a tale so accurately and so well.

3. *The loss of a pet.* Losing a pet can be as devastating as losing a family member, yet this loss is one of the least understood.

Many people consider pets as mere belongings. Some people fear animals, are allergic to them, or just don't like them. They have no idea of the affection, companionship, and love that can develop between a person and a pet.

Children, childless couples, people who live alone, and older adults often grow attached to animals and consider them members of the family. Sometimes a pet is a link with the past, is the only other surviving member of a family in crisis, or has been at a person's side through trauma.

For these people, a life-style as well as a friend has been lost. No longer does the dog expect his exercise walk promptly at 7:00 a.m. The cat is not there to rub their ankles when they come home from work.

The loss is deepened by guilt when one must decide on euthanasia for a sick pet. When moving owners cannot take a pet along, or a new baby forces them to relocate the animal, they feel loss.

All these losses cause grief that is complicated by the fear of what others will say. Comments such as "It was only a pet!" or "Why don't you just get another one?" can hurt deeply and make bereaved pet owners feel they cannot trust others with their feelings.

Who Says Winners Never Lose?

INTANGIBLE LOSSES

Loss comes by other avenues as well. When a loved one runs away from home, joins a cult, is sent to prison, slips into a coma, becomes mentally ill, or is in the custody of a hostile ex-spouse—we can experience deep grief.

Counselor Ira Tanner explains,

> Some of the most excruciating grief I have ever witnessed has been on occasions where not death but ordinary events have separated people: loss of a son or daughter to the ravages of drugs, bankruptcy, loss of trust within a vintage relationship. Ann, for instance, upon being told her son was institutionalized for alcoholism, inquired over and over of several close friends, "Is it really true?" To herself she wondered if she was dreaming. But the passing of time coupled with persistent and patient validation helped to gradually make the loss real to her. "It would have been easier," she mourned, "had he actually died."[5]

When David became king, he commanded that his wife Michal (Saul's daughter) be returned to him. While he had been in hiding from Saul, Saul had married her to Paltiel.

Paltiel was so distraught at losing Michal he "went with her, weeping behind her all the way" (2 Sam. 3:16) and didn't turn back until the commander of the army ordered him to return home.

For most people, the loss of a loved one is the most difficult loss of all. Scripture records many who suffered in this way and their own unique ways of dealing with it.

When your world is shattered because you have lost a loved one, remember that the heavenly Father understands your heartache. His only Son died of torture. He knows how you feel and longs to comfort you in your grief.

Loss of Loved Ones

TIME TO CONSIDER

1. Have you ever lost a loved one to death? What was the impact on you?

2. Have you experienced loss of a loved one to something other than death? Explain its effect on you.

3. As one who lost his Son to death, how might God comfort us?

4. How has loss of a loved one enabled you to empathize with another who has faced the same pain?

7

Loss of Health

We all experience the loss of health at one time or another. Whether a simple cold or a rare cancer, ill-health brings loss of comfort, ability, money, continuation of our life-style, and in critical cases, loss of life itself.

After losing all his possessions and children, "Job did not sin by charging God with wrongdoing" (Job 1:22). Still, Satan insisted if Job lost his health, "he will surely curse you to your face" (Job 2:5). Go ahead, the Lord said, make him sick, but just don't take his life. Satan covered Job's body with boils.

Most Bible scholars agree that the boils were probably a symptom of a more serious disease. One points out that Job's skin lesions could have been caused by any number of ailments; from parasitic infections to dermatitis herpetiformis.[1] Another suggests "the disease of Job was a species

Who Says Winners Never Lose?

of black leprosy commonly called *Elephantiasis*."[2]

Whatever the scientific cause, Job was so sick he thought he was going to die. "My body is clothed with worms and scabs, my skin is broken and festering" (7:5). "I am nothing but skin and bones" (19:20). "Night pierces my bones; my gnawing pains never rest" (30:17). "My skin grows black and peels; my body burns with fever" (30:30). "I have been allotted months of futility, and nights of misery have been assigned to me. When I lie down I think, 'How long before I get up?'" (7:3,4).

Job speaks of himself in third person. "His flesh wastes away to nothing, and his bones, once hidden, now stick out. His soul draws near to the pit, and his life to the messengers of death" (33:21, 22).

LOSS OF PHYSICAL HEALTH

Mallon's cancer diagnosis profoundly affected our entire family. We made scores of seventy-mile trips to Children's Hospital for treatments and hospitalizations. Not only were we faced with his imminent death, our household routine was shattered.

After the doctors implanted a hyper-alimentation line in his body to reduce the number of needles needed for chemotherapy, I had to learn a daily home-care routine to prevent a fatal blood clot from forming.

Aimee could no longer play with him. One family, convinced cancer was contagious, cut us off completely for years.

Although insurance covered many expenses, we still had to pay thousands of dollars in medical bills and received no help for daily needs. Once, I had no money to buy meals in the hospital cafeteria and ate baby food sent to Mallon's room in error (he was breast-feeding).

People from all walks of life suffer illness. Even in

Loss of Health

biblical times, elevated social position did not guarantee good health. We read of illness suffered by Jacob, Elisha, Miriam, the Syrian kings Ben-Hadad and Naaman, Jewish king Hezekiah, and Israelite prince Abijah.

Healing the sick was an important part of Jesus' ministry. Scripture states "this was to fulfill what was spoken through the prophet Isaiah: 'He took up our infirmities and carried our diseases'" (Matt. 8:17).

Loss of health meant loss of social standing (lepers and the ceremonially unclean woman who bled), loss of ability to earn a living (the blind and lame), even loss of life (Lazarus and Tabitha).

Today, with all our scientific advances, good health is still a valuable treasure. Ill-health and injury bring confinement, avoidance by others, burdensome medical bills, pain, and side effects of medicine.

Sometimes we lose a body part to accident or disease. Whether an external limb or an internal organ, we grieve the loss. Our concept of our bodies can be drastically altered following amputation; and the operation can cause people to "feel" the severed limb as if it were still there.

Becky Conway, daughter of authors Jim and Sally Conway, lost a leg because of a tumor when she was fifteen. She handles the loss with determination and a sense of humor, delighting audiences with stories of children in supermarkets who say things like, "Mommy, she's broken her leg off. She must not have drunk her milk!"

In dealing with her loss, Becky had the same struggles as everyone else yet can now say, "I do believe God allows certain things to happen to us—natural things—to make us into people we should be."

Who Says Winners Never Lose?

LOSS OF MENTAL HEALTH

My friend Peggy tells of her ninety-year-old great grandma trying to adjust to a move.

After she was settled in her wheelchair, her fingers fidgeted with the edge of the cushion. She searched the folds in her skirt and picked at the inside corners of her cardigan pockets. Seeing her anxiety, her daughter asked, "Are you missing something?"

"Oh, yes." She sighed. "I believe I've lost my mind, and it was a perfectly good one, too."

Underneath the humor, simmer frustration and pain. Loss of mental health is not only a hardship for the victim, but also for friends and family. Mentally ill people often act in socially unacceptable ways. Their illness can make it difficult for them to carry out everyday tasks or to get along with other people.

Some mentally ill people react to their condition by blaming others. Some withdraw from reality. In severe cases, mentally ill people may cause physical harm to themselves or to others.

Mark's gospel tells about a man who lived naked among the tombs and cut himself with stones. When Jesus cast out the demons that caused his mental illness, the people who came to investigate found the man "sitting there, dressed and in his right mind" (Mark 5:15).

Ill-health and other losses not responded to correctly can bring on depression. One psychotherapist describes depression as "a mourning process gone askew . . . . Mourning is an emotional process in which we work through, and ultimately accept, a loss . . . . The person who is mourning in a healthy manner recognizes there has been a loss. While he is working through this loss, he still perceives the world and himself realistically and is able to follow through on

Loss of Health

his daily routines. The depressed person, however, is completely preoccupied with the loss, with the feeling of sadness and grief."[3]

THE COMPLICATION OF STRESS

Two researchers have developed a test which lists forty-three events that cause stress.[4] Using Job's wife as an example, let's use this test to see what deep loss can do to a person's stress level.

LIFE CHANGE SCALE

Rank		Mean Value	Job's Wife's Score
1.	Death of spouse	100	
2.	Divorce	73	
3.	Marital separation	65	
4.	Jail term	63	
5.	Death of close family member	63 (x10)	630
6.	Personal injury or illness	53	
7.	Marriage	50	
8.	Fired at work	47	
9.	Marital reconciliation	45	
10.	Retirement	45	
11.	Change in health of family member	44	44
12.	Pregnancy	40	
13.	Sex difficulties	39	
14.	Gain new family member	39	
15.	Business readjustment	39	
16.	Change in financial state	38	38
17.	Death of close friend	37	
18.	Change to different line of work	36	
19.	Change in number of arguments with spouse	35	
20.	Mortgage over $50,000	31	
21.	Foreclosure of mortgage or loan	30	

Who Says Winners Never Lose?

LIFE CHANGE SCALE (continued)

Rank		Mean Value	Job's Wife's Score
22.	Change in responsibilities at work	29	
23.	Son or daughter leaving home	29	
24.	Trouble with in-laws	29	
25.	Outstanding personal achievement	28	
26.	Wife begins or stops work	26	
27.	Begin or end school	26	
28.	Change in living conditions	25	<u>25</u>
29.	Revision of personal habits	24	<u>24</u>
30.	Trouble with boss	23	
31.	Change in work hours or conditions	20	
32.	Change in residence	20	
33.	Change in schools	20	
34.	Change in recreation	19	
35.	Change in church activities	19	
36.	Change in social activities	18	<u>18</u>
37.	Mortgage or loan less than $50,000	17	
38.	Change in sleeping habits	16	
39.	Change in number of family get-togethers	15	<u>15</u>
40.	Change in eating habits	15	
41.	Vacation	13	
42.	Christmas	12	
43.	Minor violations of the law	11	
	Total		**<u>794</u>**

A score of 150 points or less on the scale within a one-year period indicates a 33 percent probability that the person tested will come down with a significant illness or suffer an accident within the next two years. A score of 150 to 300 points raises the chance to 50–50. More than 300 points ranks a 90 percent chance of illness or injury.

Loss of Health

Although this list is geared to modern culture, some of life's experiences remain constant as stress producers. Perhaps we did not compute all the possible points Job's wife "earned," but even those we know add up to a staggering score of 794.

An evil woman? Perhaps. But I think she was a normal human caught in the vise of loss. Squeezed dry of all her treasures, she lashed out at whoever was around her. By its very nature, deep loss affects our mental and even physical health to some degree.

LOSS OF THE HEALTH OF A LOVED ONE

Who took care of Job on that ash heap? Who brought food to the three friends who sat with him? Most of the servants had been killed along with the livestock, and now that Job and his wife were poor, it's possible the rest had left. I believe that Job's wife was the caregiver. She prepared food and drink and brought water for washing.

While scripture does not specifically state that's what happened, it does tell us of other caregivers, the most famous of whom is the Good Samaritan. In caring for the injured stranger, the Samaritan traveler gave of his time, effort, and money to restore the man to health. Jesus instructed his listeners, "Go and do likewise" (Luke 10:37).

Aging Parents

A growing number of adults find themselves in the "sandwich generation"—individuals who care for both their children and their aging parents. Surveys indicate that the role of caregiver for older parents most often falls to women. In fact, daughters are twice as likely as sons to become primary caregivers. Even when the son decides to care for his parents, the daughter-in-law usually inherits the actual caregiving tasks.

Who Says Winners Never Lose?

At these times, adult children discover a deeper meaning to "honor thy father and thy mother." It requires love, sacrifice, and patience during trying times in a child–parent relationship.

Spouses

By the time doctors discovered our friend George's prostate cancer, it had spread beyond control. He was adamant about spending his last days at home.

At first his wife Marian was devastated. "I thought we'd have the rest of our lives together, and one thinks of that as being a long time," she told me. "But he was the one who was sick. So I turned my attention to bolstering him physically and emotionally."

As George grew weaker, Marian took on the responsibility for their business in addition to her homemaking duties and his increasing health care needs. Each responsibility was time-consuming.

"It changed our lives completely. Dealing with his illness was very much like running a business," she observed. Marian's responsibility included scheduling and working with many people coming into the home—doctors, nurses, and other health professionals. After George was confined to bed, physiotherapists, social workers, and other helpers joined the daily parade.

During the last six months, when he was totally bedbound, Marian hardly ever left the house. Occasionally someone would sit with him for a couple of hours so she could attend a support group.

"Losing his health meant a great load on me," she says, "both emotionally and physically—without a partner to help. It was like being alone before I was a widow."

The burdens placed on the spouses of the sick or injured are innumerable. While the invalid undeniably suffers, we

Loss of Health

shouldn't forget the caring loved one who battles fatigue, time pressure, and guilt. Such people need to receive much love, support, and encouragement.

Marian survived the ordeal because others helped her. "I couldn't have made it through the last year without the physical and emotional support of two or three friends," she said.

When Jesus told his disciples that when they visited the sick it was as if they visited him, he meant more than simply stopping by for a ten-minute chat. The Greek word he used for visit, *episkeptomai*, means "to inspect, to look upon, care for, exercise oversight." When we help care for those who have lost their health, Jesus says it is as if we cared for Jesus himself.

Whether our loss is our own physical or mental health or the health of a loved one, the burden can be difficult to bear alone. We need each other. Perhaps in this loss, as much as in any other, we are to "carry each other's burdens, and in this way you will fulfill the law of Christ" (Gal. 6:2).

TIME TO CONSIDER

1. Remember a time when you were sick. What other losses did you experience along with your loss of health?

2. Think of the events in your life over the past year and compute your score on the *Life Change Scale*. What do the results tell you about your lifestyle?

3. If your stress score is high, how might you lower it? If your score is low, what factors contributed?

4. If you have been a caregiver to an ill loved one, what helped you through the difficult time? If you've never been a caregiver, what strategies for survival might you employ if you're ever in the position to be one?

8
Loss of Dignity and Other Intangibles

Family and friends avoided Job and his wife because they thought the two were being punished by God. Job lamented to his three comforters that God "has alienated my brothers from me; my acquaintances are completely estranged from me. My kinsmen have gone away; my friends have forgotten me" (Job 19:13,14). No doubt those avoiding Job also steered clear of his wife.

Not until the end of the trial, after the Lord gave Job twice as much as he had before, did his brothers, sisters, and acquaintances come to comfort him (Job 42:11).

While Job now holds a place of high regard in mankind's estimation, Job's wife has never regained her position of honor. She lost everyone's respect when she uttered her anguished outburst.

Matthew Henry said, "She was spared to him, when the

rest of his comforts were taken away, for this purpose, to be a troubler and tempter to him." Augustine called her "the adjutant of the devil," and compared her with Eve in tempting her husband to forsake his Creator. John Calvin said she was "an instrument of Satan."

THE LOSS OF DIGNITY AND SELF-ESTEEM

Loss of dignity can be as devastating. Several years ago some high school boys played a practical joke on a schoolmate—they pulled his pants down in front of a crowd. Unable to handle his loss of dignity, he went home and hanged himself.

Sometimes a person reacts to loss of dignity by overcompensation, such as working hard to develop good points to make up for the area of weakness.

Greg Louganis is the first diver in Olympic history to win gold medals in both springboard and platform competition. In 1988, he received the Olympic Spirit Award as the most inspiring athlete of the Games.

Greg has not always received applause. When he was young, classmates made fun of his dark Samoan complexion with taunts of "nigger." They laughed at him when he was called upon to answer in class because he stuttered and had dyslexia.

"I didn't speak much as a kid because everybody laughed at me," he told an interviewer just before the 1988 Olympics. "It was so frustrating. I decided to direct all my time and energy into something I could be proficient in. I wanted to show people I could do something . . . so I totally honed in on my physical attributes."

His coach, Dr. Sammy Lee, has more in common with Greg than diving skills. "I know all about how cruel people can be," he said. "How would you like to be a five-foot-tall Korean kid living on the California coast right after the

Loss of Dignity and Other Intangibles

1941 Pearl Harbor attack, and every day have people calling the FBI to lock up 'the dirty little Jap spy' hanging around the local swimming pools, masquerading as a diver?"

Not only did Dr. Lee compensate for his loss of dignity by winning gold medals at the 1948 London and 1952 Helsinki Olympics, he went on to become a successful ear, nose, and throat specialist. However, scars from his earlier loss of dignity will always remain.

Jesus ministered to everyone who would receive him, but it was the "common people" who "heard him gladly" (Mark 12:37 KJV). He treated society's second class citizens—women, tax collectors, fishermen, lepers, beggars, the poor—as people of worth. He looked beyond the value that society had ascribed to them and saw their true value.

When you struggle with situations that seem to rob you of your dignity and sense of value, remember that God values each person's soul as worth more than the entire world (Mark 8:36).

The prophet Zechariah says that God so values his people that "whoever touches you touches the apple of his eye" (Zech. 2:8). Since the apple is the pupil of the eye, God is saying that he values us highly and hurts when we suffer loss.

THE LOSS OF SECURITY AND FREEDOM

1. *Through loss of income.* Several years ago a friend was laid off his job and couldn't find another one although he was young and well-qualified. He believed God would provide for their needs, but his wife wasn't so sure.

"Women are security-minded," she told me later. "My husband would say, 'The Lord will provide,' and I'd say, 'When? How? Where? I don't see it. The bill is due tomorrow.'"

Who Says Winners Never Lose?

Looking back, she remembers miracles such as when their cupboard remained full weeks after they had shopped for groceries. "There were other similar incidents; but because I hurt so much, I didn't see many of them," she said.

Her loss of security left scars even though her husband has a good job today. "I still have fears about money after all these years. With that fear comes guilt. Everybody says, 'Just trust the Lord.' It's so hard, though."

2. *Through loss of familiar surroundings.* We can lose security and freedom when we change careers or enter retirement or whenever we move away from familiar surroundings, even for positive reasons. Gone is our network of car mechanics, hairdressers, baby-sitters, our nodding friendships with the librarian, butcher, bank teller. Loss of familiar surroundings is one reason it's difficult for older people to leave their own homes and enter retirement centers, even when such moves are necessary because of failing health and strength.

Freshman college students traditionally experience this loss at the beginning of their academic year. Children whose families move frequently often struggle in school.

The longer we stay in one place—home, job, school, church—the deeper we plant roots. Pulling them up always means some degree of loss in stability. In severe cases, people can wilt from lack of nourishment.

3. *When living in limbo.* We lose security and freedom when we wait for an impending crisis to break such as waiting through a terminal illness or an unresolved family crisis.

Living in limbo means staying close to home and not making long-term decisions. No doubt Job's wife experienced this as she listened to her husband debate with his friends at the local dump. What about her future? Would

Loss of Dignity and Other Intangibles

Job die after all? Was he really a sinner as the men insisted? Had God forgotten them?

Susan Whitehead learned about living in uncertainty when her husband arranged to work overseas. They did everything they could to prepare for the move and then waited in a holding pattern for the call telling them things were ready.

As time passed and no call came, they were faced with decisions. Should they plant a garden? Should the children try out for the school play or the softball team? Should they make holiday plans knowing they might have to cancel at the last minute? As more time went by, they experienced anxiety, insomnia, fatigue, and depression.

Through it all, Susan discovered that life at its most secure is still a limbo of sorts. "We are presumptuous to think we have control over our future," she said. "What we do have—the only bit of life we can count on—is this moment."[1]

We can also lose security and freedom when we wait indefinitely for a happy event to take place. Pregnant women near their due dates cannot travel far from home. Prolonged waiting to fill the empty nursery can bring anxiety.

4. *Through imprisonment.* People lose freedom when they are put into prison. Often we think that, since criminals deserve punishment, we need not show sympathy. Jesus, however, encouraged us to have compassion on them. He said that whenever we visit prisoners, it's as if we visit Jesus himself (Matt. 25:36–40).

Remember too that not everyone in prison is guilty. Just as many early believers were unjustly jailed (John the Baptist, Paul, Silas, Peter, John the apostle, Jesus), so are thousands of believers imprisoned in godless countries today because they follow Christ. Some people, framed

Who Says Winners Never Lose?

by someone else or victims of circumstantial evidence, serve sentences for crimes they did not commit.

Imprisonment brings other losses. Violence is often a threat. Privacy, dignity, and reputation are lost. Women inmates cannot be with their children—even newborns.

People who thrive in spite of these conditions do so by determining not to get bitter, by praying, and by choosing to thank God for any gifts. One tortured woman in a Chinese dungeon kept her sanity by watching a busy spider who crept into her cell and tenaciously spun intricate webs. It encouraged her not to give up in spite of her hopeless situation.

Whether we lose our security and freedom through poverty, moving, imprisonment, or waiting for an event to happen, following Paul's advice will help us cope. "Whatever you do, work at it with all your heart, as working for the Lord, not for men, since you know that you will receive an inheritance from the Lord as a reward. It is the Lord Christ you are serving" (Col. 3:23,24).

Ultimately, our security and freedom come from God alone. Jesus told his disciples, "Therefore I tell you, do not worry about your life, what you will eat; or about your body, what you will wear." He reminded them that the ravens don't plant, reap, or store food, yet God feeds them. "And how much more valuable you are than birds!" (Luke 12:22–24).

THE LOSS OF DREAMS AND AMBITIONS

1. *Through career upheaval.* Most major losses damage our dreams for the future. Cynthia Clawson experienced this in 1983 when she was on top of the Christian music world. Her song, "Come Celebrate Jesus," was number one on the charts. She had twice been named the Gospel Music Association's Female Vocalist of the Year and had

Loss of Dignity and Other Intangibles

received one Grammy and two Dove awards.

Then, without notice, her record company shut its doors; she and her husband Ragan learned they were embroiled in a lawsuit. Songs they had written for the past ten years were no longer in the marketplace. Cynthia's lawyer advised her not to perform, record, or publish any more music until the legal entanglement cleared up.

In mourning the loss of her dreams and aspirations, Cynthia battled rage, anger, and hate. Ragan identified with Job's wife. "I wanted to curse God," he admitted.[2]

Sometimes the loss of dreams is permanent. Other times, our dreams are reshaped into a new hope that God delights in fulfilling. When Cynthia Clawson was finally able to sign a new contract, she said, "This album is truly a reflection of what Ragan and I have been through and how we have come out victorious!"

2. *Through infertility.* Infertile couples suffer many losses. Not only do they face the loss of a dream for a family, fertility treatments are expensive, and adoption can cost thousands of dollars.

Discussing intimate details with doctors and scheduling romance quickly brings loss of privacy and spontaneity. Couples also suffer from prying questions and unasked-for advice.

Infertility can threaten a woman's self-image and cause her to envy or even resent others who conceive easily. Reminders of her childless state are everywhere—women's magazines full of ads and articles about mothering, babies at the park, church bulletins requesting nursery volunteers. Outsiders almost always ask the wife, not the husband, if they have children.

No matter what the reason for the loss of dreams and ambitions, we must remember that God is concerned with our future. " 'For I know the plans I have for you,' declares the Lord, 'plans to prosper you and not to harm you, plans to give you hope and a future'" (Jer. 29:11).

THE LOSS OF YOUTH AND BEAUTY

1. *Through aging.* Calling beauty "the gold coin of human worth" in our society, Dr. James Dobson states that "the more attractive a person is in his youth, the more painful is the aging process."[3]

As pounds, wrinkles, balding, and bifocals creep up on us, we collectively spend billions of dollars to slow our losses. We may tease the birthday person on his or her fortieth birthday by sending sympathy cards and black balloons, but behind the laughter, we imply that growing older is a tragedy.

God views aging differently. His word states, "Gray hair is a crown of splendor; it is attained by a righteous life" (Prov. 16:31).

2. *Through disfigurement.* Various wars returned thousands of our young men with wounds in both body and soul. One, Dave Roever, almost burned to death when a phosphorous grenade exploded in his hand. Even though he swam from the boat to the bank of the Vam Co Tay River, he was still burning from the phosphorous when medics put him on a stretcher. Thinking he was dead, they loaded another wounded man into the helicopter first. Meanwhile, Dave caught the stretcher on fire, and when the medics picked it up, it ripped open and he fell out onto his head.

Dave was aware they thought he had died, and he didn't want them to poke his dogtags into his gums—the usual procedure with corpses—so he croaked, "Medic," and badly scared the crew.

After working on him in a MASH unit, they sent him to a hospital in Japan where he learned he had suffered third-degree burns over forty percent of his upper body and had

Loss of Dignity and Other Intangibles

lost sixty pounds of flesh and body fluids. His right cheek, ear, and nostril had been blown off. His right eye was gray, and the eyelid was gone. Organs showed through a hole in his chest.

A medic was foolish enough to grant his request for a mirror. "When I looked into that mirror I was struck with a lightning bolt of soul-destroying pain," Dave said later. "My soul seemed to shrivel up, to collapse in on itself, to be sucked into a black hole of despair. I was left with an indescribable and terrifying emptiness. I was alone the way souls in hell must feel alone.... I was overwhelmed by fears of rejection. I found myself utterly repulsive. I could not and would not identify myself with the monster in the mirror. How could anybody else?"[4]

After a year of treatment, when Dave was well enough to leave the hospital and step into the "real" world, his identity became an overwhelming issue. "The bad side of my face looked like the ball at the tip of a roll-on deodorant bottle," he said. In addition to being smooth and featureless, his face was blood red from new skin, and half his mouth was sewn together.

In the hall he passed a mother with twins. The children screamed, "Mommy, what is it? Mommy, what is it?"

In spite of the devastating loss of appearance, Dave now considers himself very fortunate. Not only did his wife stay with him after the accident, she unconditionally accepted his disfigured appearance. Many other injured veterans were not so lucky.

Loss of personal appearance can be a devastating loss, whether from injury, disease, or the simple erosion of time.

God tells us his perspective of the importance of physical appearance. "The Lord does not look at the things man looks at. Man looks at the outward appearance, but the Lord looks at the heart" (1 Sam. 16:7). Scripture also says,

Who Says Winners Never Lose?

"Charm is deceptive, and beauty is fleeting; but a woman who fears the Lord is to be praised" (Prov. 31:30).

MISCELLANEOUS LOSSES

We often feel loss at the end of vacation, summer, or the Christmas season. We sense loss when the earth is damaged by oil spills or acid rain. Though we may be removed from the victims, we grieve the loss of life due to famine, earthquakes, abortions, or serial killers.

We are brought up to believe that being a good sport in competition means not grieving when we lose. However, losers in athletic contests as well as games such as cards, badminton, or horseshoes suffer from loss. Without at least a few wins now and then, people usually stop competing to minimize the damage to their self-esteem.

That we did not "win" the war in Vietnam and, as a result, rejected those who risked their lives to fight it shows that entire nations can be adversely affected by competitive loss.

The loss may be trivial. When I was a girl, we used to watch for an arch in a row of birches lining the freeway on our way to the big city. A tree trunk or large branch formed an unusual rainbow shape that joined the trunk of one tree to the next. Not only was it a curiosity among visitors, it had been featured in "Ripley's Believe It or Not."

Then someone cut the arch for firewood, its parent trees died, and outraged citizens voiced their anger in letters to the newspaper editor. The curiosity of nature had been part of the area's culture, and people grieved the irreplaceable loss.

When his Cub Scout trip got rained out, Josh cried. Not understanding his grief, his father said, "It's no big deal. There will be other camp-outs."

For more than twenty years, Mrs. Selkirk sat in the same

Loss of Dignity and Other Intangibles

pew every Sunday. One morning she found someone else sitting in her spot—and she grieved all day. When she mentioned it to the ladies at the missionary prayer circle on Thursday, they chuckled behind their coffee cups.

While small losses may at times prepare us for larger losses, sometimes the little ones hurt the most because they are the most misunderstood. If we have been already wounded by a major loss, these little griefs can inflict great pain, especially when several happen at the same time.

In counseling grieving people, Ira Tanner has learned that "we do not see eye to eye on what constitutes 'loss,' but we should always attempt to understand *feelings of loss* in others."[5] Somehow, bearing these little losses as well as the big ones is easier when people around us understand what we are going through.

Intangible losses are as real as any other kind. Jesus said that part of his reason for coming was "to proclaim freedom for the prisoners . . . to release the oppressed, to proclaim the year of the Lord's favor" (Luke 4:18,19).

TIME TO CONSIDER

1. If you have ever felt a loss of dignity, tell how it affected your self-esteem. What makes loss of dignity a difficult loss with which to cope?

2. If you were nurtured back to a sense of wholeness, how was it done? If not, why not? What truths have you learned that you might someday apply to another time of loss of dignity?

3. Why is loss of freedom and security so unsettling to our sense of balance? Analyze whether it is easy for you to adjust to changes or if you tend to cling to that which appears stable. Why?

Who Says Winners Never Lose?

4. If you have ever mourned the death of a dream, describe your grief and how you worked it through to resolution. If you haven't yet resolved it, what are you learning during this painful time?

9

Loss of Faith in God

Shortly before discovering Mallon had cancer, we received teaching that God always heals us if we have enough faith. The proponents of this belief pointed out that sickness and death are the work of Satan (Luke 13:16; Acts 10:38). Since the purpose of Jesus' coming was to destroy Satan's works (1 John 3:8), believers in Jesus can *expect* to be free from illness.

We'd always believed in divine healing, but these people insisted healing was our inherent right as children of God. Anyone who remained sick was not claiming that right, but was living in defeat.

It seemed too coincidental to me that Mallon's tumor was discovered just as we learned these new "truths." Convinced God was testing my faith, I determined he would find no doubt in *my* heart.

Who Says Winners Never Lose?

Even though each doctor's report grew more pessimistic, I refused to prepare myself for the possibility of Mallon's death. What if God should view such thoughts as lack of faith? No, if it depended on my faith, Mallon was not going to die.

Mallon's condition grew worse, and he slipped into a coma the day before his first birthday. So, on the next day, his birthday, intravenous tubes poked his body from head to foot. A respirator pumped his little lungs, and fluids had so bloated his body, he didn't even look human.

Angry and confused, I cried out to God. "Why haven't you healed him yet? You know I haven't doubted. How long must he suffer before you heal him?"

Deep within, I heard God's still, small voice. "You must give him to me."

This is the last condition God requires to heal Mallon, I thought. All the doctors and nurses would be amazed at God's mighty power, especially since they said he now had irreversible brain damage. "All right," I whispered. "I give him to you."

At 11:00 p.m., a nurse urged my husband and me to lie down. "We'll tell you if there is any change," she said. One hour later, she touched my shoulder. "Mallon just died."

Questions swirled in my groggy brain as we rode the elevator back upstairs. Had God deceived me? Did his word *not* promise healing after all? Most important, if my beliefs were erroneous, why hadn't God revealed it to me?

My arms were abruptly empty and so was my soul. On top of the pain of losing a child, I struggled with fading faith.

I had climbed out on a limb and watched God cut it. "I'm not afraid," I had told him, "I know you'll stop in time, or at least catch me when I fall." But when the limb broke off, I plunged to the ground and lay crushed, broken,

Loss of Faith in God

and hurting.

Worst of all, I couldn't tell anyone how I felt. It was understood that truly spiritual Christians don't admit that they feel God has failed them.

A short time later, a young minister spoke in our church. "Has God ever failed anyone here?" he asked, scanning the crowd. I felt like raising my hand and saying, "Yoo hoo, over here," but, of course, I didn't. He continued with his message, confident he had made his point, but I could no longer listen. Was I the only one who felt this way? Had everyone else's prayer received an answer? Why had God ignored mine?

Though my faith was crushed, I knew I could not turn away from God. Simon Peter's words became mine. "Lord, to whom shall we go? You have the words of eternal life" (John 6:68). I survived by clinging to the end of my rope of faith and begging God not to send anything else along that would knock me into the abyss below.

A COMMON RESPONSE

I have since discovered that I am not alone in the way I responded to deep loss. When Pastor Jim Conway's daughter, Becky, faced leg amputation, he told her "You're not going to have your leg off. I believe God and what he has said about prayer. I'm absolutely convinced about it. We're going to ask God for healing."

He asked the doctor to check the leg carefully before amputating. "I believe God's going to come through," he said.

When the doctor came out of surgery and told Jim that he'd had to amputate, Jim was shattered. "I lost God," he said later. "In anger I found myself beating the wall, saying, 'Where were you God? Where are you? What is prayer?'

Who Says Winners Never Lose?

"If I had been a plumber, I could have gone back to work the next day and fixed pipes and God could have continued to be irrelevant. But my job was standing before people, telling them that the Bible is true.... I was supposed to go back and tell people that God is a magnificent God who honors prayer—and it wasn't happening."[1]

Some Nazi concentration camp survivors lost their faith in God. To them, the experience was final proof that God did not care about the human plight. Jews were especially susceptible to loss of faith because they had been raised to believe they were a chosen people.

Others lost their faith just by learning about the tragedy. Novelist and short-story writer Hugh Nissenson was by his own admission "not an observant Jew, but I was a deeply believing one. I believed . . . that God was working in history, that a redemptive process was, in some mysterious way, despite the Holocaust, going on."

Attending the Barbie war crimes trial changed his views. "It was the problem of the death of children," he said. "What obsessed me was the forty-four Jewish children being kept in the house at Izieu whom Barbie sent to Auschwitz to die. And my belief in a personal God, the idea that a God could have any particular interest in me as an individual, was dramatically eroded, and eventually cracked, as a result of that first trial.... I could no longer reconcile ultimately my belief that God was working in history.... I could no longer reconcile that with the reality of evil."[2]

It need not take tragedy on the scale of the holocaust to puncture trust in God. When one husband exhibited the classic signs of a mid-life crisis—sports car, mod clothes, and an affair with a much younger woman—his wife did all the things her Christian friends told her to do so that God would restore her marriage. Her husband divorced her anyway and married the other woman.

She became resentful and bitter and declared that "religion" didn't work. "If God doesn't care about me and my problems, what good is it to serve him?" she asked.

Even ministers can lose faith in God when faced with bitter loss. Joseph Parker, who made London's City Temple world famous, publicly declared that doubt never bothered him. Then his wife died.

"In that dark hour I became almost an atheist. How could I be otherwise—my chief joy taken from me? . . . O the Gethsemane bitterness! . . . I had secretly prayed God to pity me by sparing her, yet he set his foot upon my prayers, and treated my petitions with contempt. If I had seen a dog in such agony as mine I would have pitied and helped the dumb beast; yet God spat upon me and cast me out as an offence."[3]

JOB'S WIFE'S LOSS OF FAITH

Job's wife is best remembered for urging her stricken husband to curse God and die. But consider that, in one day, this well-to-do mother of ten became poor and childless and then stared the spectre of widowhood in the face, and we realize she need not have been an evil woman to say what she did.

When we encounter someone in the pain of loss who appears to be shaking a fist in God's face, let's take care not to judge hastily. Even in the seemingly clear-cut matter of this woman's anguished cry, "Curse God and die!" (Job 2:9), there is some controversy.

The primary meaning of the Hebrew word *berekh* is "bless." Some Bible scholars believe she thought Job was near death and said, "Bless God and die."

Since Job chided her not to speak as the foolish women, he probably understood her to mean it euphemistically (as did Satan in 1:11 and 2:5). Some feel she could have had good intentions. Watching her righteous husband writhe in agony, she may have thought a quick death would be better than a slow one. And since people of that day thought that God would strike dead anyone who cursed him, she prescribed for Job a theological method of committing suicide.

While I personally don't believe these views are correct, they emphasize the importance of looking at the loser's point of view. I suspect Job understood her better than do most of us. Notice he did not say, "I would be better off without you!" as many people suggest. He simply warned her not to speak as the foolish women—a gentle rebuke in time of great mutual grief.

Perhaps he understood that, burdened with sudden poverty, severe bereavement, and the responsibilities of caring almost single-handedly for a sick husband, she was no doubt filled with seething anger. She was angry with God for letting all this happen and angry with herself because she couldn't accept and believe God the same way Job did.

If any other person had dealt with her and her loved ones in such a manner, her human response would have been to retaliate. She could not see or touch God, but Job was within reach, handy for her to lash out at and a constant reminder that they had both been targeted for suffering.

VICTIMS OF THE FAITH MOVEMENT

The emphasis on faith teaching in recent years has blessed many people. Marvelous answers to prayer and untold blessings have come into their lives.

For others, it has meant loss of their faith in God.

As with any biblical truth, distortions and excesses are possible. Certain ministers have built large followings by telling people what they want to hear and soft-pedaling the

Loss of Faith in God

more unpopular parts of the gospel.

"Live right, confess victory, give your tithes and offerings to this ministry, and blessings will overtake you," they say. "Rebuke the devil, and he will never be able to touch you. We are *more* than conquerors in Christ Jesus!"

While I don't wish to downgrade the importance of faith in our Christian walk, I am concerned about the victims of unbalanced teaching. When these people experience severe loss, it raises questions in their minds about the nature of God. Didn't they follow the formula? Wasn't God bound to come through with his part of the bargain? Is there any point in trusting God, after all?

The key, again, is balance. The same Bible that promises that God always hears our prayers, also talks about suffering "grief in all kinds of trials" (1 Pet. 1:6) and tells us to consider it pure joy "whenever you face trials of many kinds, because you know that the testing of your faith develops perseverance" (James 1:2).

The same New Testament that tells us "prayer offered in faith will make the sick person well" (James 5:15) relates Paul's futile struggle to be free from his thorn in the flesh (2 Cor. 12:7–9).

We are to believe God for healing, protection, and deliverance. We must also remember that sometimes God allows us to suffer for a higher purpose. His refusal to deliver on demand does not mean that he has failed us.

WHEN WE LASH OUT AT GOD

Becky Smith Greer's husband, son, brother-in-law, and nephew were victims of a plane crash two days after Christmas. Although a Christian, she was unprepared to handle the tragedy.

"Everything that I'd ever believed in was destroyed," she said later. "I could not understand how a God who loved

Who Says Winners Never Lose?

me could allow my family to be cut in half."[4]

In the fall of that year, she and her daughter were invited to a band concert dedicated to the memory of her director husband. As the music swelled over the crowd she cried out, "God, I hate you, I hate you, I hate you!"

Feeling as if everything she had believed in was gone, she bought an easy translation of the Bible, joined a Bible study, and prepared to start over. The long road to recovery began.

"I learned when you're hurting, you need some arms around you." she said. "We don't need to be superhuman, we just need to allow ourselves the freedom to grieve, then allow our friends to love us. It's not an overnight, magic thing. It took me about two-and-a-half years to move through the grieving process."

Becky was able to comprehend God's love toward her because people loved her.

Well-known author Sheldon Vanauken was so crushed by the death of his wife Davy that he rejected God.

> The world was still empty without Davy, and now God seemed to have withdrawn, too. My sense of desolation increased. God could not be as loving as He was supposed to be, or—the other alternative. One sleepless night, drawing on to morning, I was overwhelmed with a sense of cosmos empty of God as well as Davy. "All right," I muttered to myself. "To hell with God. I'm not going to believe this damned rubbish any more. Lies, all lies. I've been had." Up I sprang and rushed out to the country. This was the end of God. Ha!
>
> And then I found I *could not* reject God. I could not. I cannot explain this. One discovers one cannot move a boulder by trying with all one's strength to do it. I

discovered—without any sudden influx of love or faith—that I could not reject Christianity. Why, I don't know. There it was. I could not. That was an end to it.

An hour later I recalled that I had *chosen* to believe, pledged my fealty to the King. That was another reason why I couldn't reject God, not without being forsworn.[5]

When we pledge to follow God, he takes our intent seriously. Our anguished cries in the depths of loss do not cause God to reconsider his end of the bargain. He has promised he will never leave nor forsake us (Josh. 1:5).

Jim Conway was blessed with friends who listened to him spill out his anger about his daughter's amputation. "I think God was so busy finding a little old lady a parking spot, he didn't have any time to save Becky's leg," he fumed. Fellow ministers listened and asked, "Is there more?"

With friends, Jim didn't have to worry about protecting his reputation as a minister or that his anger would cause them to stumble.

"The world understands the importance of catharsis," he says, "getting out all the green junk. In Christian circles we say if you're living a victorious life, you keep all the green stuff inside. But it's important to let it spill out. People say, 'Shh, don't say those things. What if God hears them?' as if God didn't know what I was thinking. Here were clear concepts in the scripture that I believed and that didn't happen. God knew I was struggling with that and who was I fooling to try to cover that up?"[6]

Paul asked "Who shall separate us from the love of Christ? Shall trouble or hardship or persecution or famine or nakedness or danger or sword? . . . No . . . . I am convinced that neither death nor life, neither angels nor

Who Says Winners Never Lose?

demons, neither the present nor the future, nor any powers, neither height nor depth, nor anything else in all creation, will be able to separate us from the love of God that is in Christ Jesus our Lord" (Rom. 8:35–39).

We often think that passage means nothing will make us leave God. It also means nothing will cause God to separate from us, no matter what we might say in our pain.

Famine, danger, and sword bring loss. Death and demons are not positive forces. God knows what we might say as a result, yet assures us we will never be separated from his love.

God understands when we are unable to trust him for a season. He is not offended by flickering faith. Though Job's wife at first lay crushed beneath her bereavements, I believe God saw a glimmer of hope and kept it alive until she was ready to take up life again. This is his true nature. "A bruised reed he will not break, and a smoldering wick he will not snuff out" (Isa.42:3).

If a flicker of life is left, God will not crush it out, regardless of our doubts.

TIME TO CONSIDER

1. Have your ever felt your faith was shaken or even destroyed because of a loss you sustained? Explain the circumstances.

2. How might God respond to us when our faith falters? Do you think he feels angry, sad, compassionate? Find several Bible verses that describe his response. Is his response always the same? Why or why not?

Part III
Search and Rescue

10

Climbing the Steep Trail Out

Grieving is mourning the lost portion of ourselves we invested in the person, place, or possession we have lost. The greater the loss, the deeper we plunge into the pit of grief. God has provided a way out which counselors refer to as *the grief process*. Each of the eleven steps in the process will lead a person back to the path of normal living.

Because no two people are alike nor are our losses identical, these steps may not come in this exact order—nor will all the steps always be necessary. On occasion it may be difficult to differentiate between the steps. A person may move back and forth between two or three before moving on.

Grieving follows a predictable pattern, and understanding it can reduce the panic of trekking through uncharted territory. Here then are the common stages

Who Says Winners Never Lose?

of grief after loss.[1]

1. *Shock and denial.* Shock blocks the pain so we can carry on during a crisis. It may last a few minutes, hours, or even days. We might observe a serene, dry-eyed widow at the funeral and say "What strong faith she has!" when in reality it's not faith but shock that carries her. When shock begins to wear off, reality sets in. Shock that lasts much longer than a week has gone beyond temporary escape and counseling is needed.

During this time, denial may occur. Several years ago, a man in our church disappeared on the river, and searchers could not find his body. For weeks, his wife refused to believe he was dead. Then she began telling friends that, even if he were dead when he was found, God would raise him up. Her life was on hold until she saw his body lowered into the grave.

After the initial shock, the wave of loss hits again and again. Some people turn to sedatives or alcohol to numb the pain, but grief counselors warn against this. Medication does not remove the pain, it only postpones dealing with it, and that makes recovery more difficult.

Ira Tanner cautions that "deciding to change locations while in shock is unwise. A cardinal rule of grief is: Never make decisions about *moving* or *money* while in shock."[2] Such decisions should be put on hold for at least a year.

2. *Expression of emotion.* Once we begin to grasp the enormity of our loss, emotions well up inside us that cry out to be released. We need to express those emotions instead of bottling them up inside.

In the next chapter, we will deal more completely with this stage of grief, and look at misconceptions in our culture that hinder expression of grief. Let me just quote here from a pastor's handbook, "If 'Jesus wept,' there is nothing particularly Christian about dry-eyed courage."[3]

3. *Bargaining.* We may try to bargain with God at this point. "If only you will heal my sister, I'll never miss church again," or "If you somehow give us back the money we lost in that deal, we'll tithe for the rest of our lives."

When bargaining doesn't work, we slip into anger or. . . .

4. *Depression.* People in loss often think no one else has ever felt as grief-stricken as they do. In a sense, this is true because every loss is different.

During this stage, we may think things we've never thought before. We may accuse God of being unfair or uncaring. David experienced this. "How long, O Lord? Will you forget me forever? How long will you hide your face from me? How long must I wrestle with my thoughts and every day have sorrow in my heart?" (Ps. 13:1,2).

When Wonda's eighteen-year-old daughter Carolyn was lost at sea in a plane crash, Wonda suppressed the grief for three years. When she finally began to face it, she slipped into a deep depression.

> I felt my whole life was in shambles. Most of the time, I was distant, listless, edgy. I made excuses to avoid social contacts, even with friends who understood. I refused to use my abilities to help anyone else. I felt inadequate to any situation. I was defensive about my rights, to be alone—to shun friends—to find fault—to die if I wanted to.
>
> When tragedy strikes a family, it does not necessarily bring the members closer together. The myth is that each needs the other more than ever before. The fact is, individual personal needs are often so great that each is absorbed with his own bag of pity, or one tries to protect the other and suffers in silence. In either case, a wedge is driven between them.[4]

Who Says Winners Never Lose?

Although this stage of depression is temporary, it is a dangerous time. In our country, large numbers of people in grief commit suicide. Others don't pull the trigger, but the spark leaves their lives. They feel isolated and alone because no one understands. Finding someone who will listen nonjudgmentally to our expressions of grief is of great importance during this stage.

5. *Physical symptoms.* The physical aspect of working through grief surprised me the most in my loss. I endured much agony while my body tried to abruptly shut off its production of milk. While my spirit felt some relief at the buckets of tears I shed, my red nose and swollen eyes did not appreciate it. I never knew facial tissue could feel so rough.

When winter came, I suffered a dozen severe colds with debilitating coughing fits. Several months into bereavement, my heart began to beat irregularly. The doctor said it was due to grieving.

If grief continues unresolved, some people may experience chest pains, temporary paralysis of a limb, vomiting, insomnia, diarrhea, trembling, or even temporary blindness.

6. *Panic.* The internal upheaval experienced during grief can cause some people to feel they are losing control or "going crazy." They panic. Lack of sleep, poor eating habits, and emotional and physical fatigue compound the problem.

Panic may be averted when we realize that, for a while, inability to concentrate on anything other than the loss is natural. Something would be wrong if we could easily put aside deep grief.

7. *Guilt.* Feelings of guilt are appropriate when we have done something that we ought not have done or have neglected to do something we should have done. But when

Climbing the Steep Trail Out

we are stricken with guilt for something for which we are not responsible, it's false guilt and can become a neurotic symptom. The key to recovery is recognizing the difference between real and false guilt and dealing with it accordingly.

If we are somehow responsible for the loss—we ran a red light, didn't lock the door, forgot to administer medication—we must ask for forgiveness and accept it.

First, we ask God, and scripture promises he will forgive (1 John 1:9). Then we ask forgiveness of anyone else who lost as the result of our action. If that person has died, this can be done by privately writing a letter asking for forgiveness. Return to a place where you feel close to the person, such as the graveside or their customary pew in church, and read the letter aloud. Even though the person is not there to hear our words, we experience release at having said them.

We may feel guilty from perceived failures in our relationship with the deceased. *I should have said "I love you." I never told her how proud I was when she graduated.* Communicate this, too, in a letter.

Near the end, when Mallon's condition deteriorated, doctors tried to control his vomiting by inserting tubes down his throat. As he writhed and screamed in the crib, his blue eyes pleaded with me, *How can you let them do this to me, Mama?* I fled to the hall and bawled.

After he died, the mental image returned to torture me. I desperately wanted him to know that I had done everything possible to save him from pain, that I would have done anything to keep him alive. One day I asked Jesus to convey that message to him, and I found tremendous comfort and release.

In dealing with false guilt, we must remember no one is perfect. If we did the best we knew how at the time, we must allow innocent errors to be blanketed under the all-forgiving grace of God. With the apostle Paul, we can say,

Who Says Winners Never Lose?

"I am still not all I should be but I am bringing all my energies to bear on this one thing: Forgetting the past and looking forward to what lies ahead" (Phil. 3:13 TLB).

8. *Anger.* Once we pass through the stage of blaming ourselves for the loss, our attention turns to others and what they should or could have done to prevent it.

Dr. Harvey Reuben works with parents who have lost children. He puts anger at the top of the list as an overwhelming stress on the marriage. "Even the best of marriages is going to be shaken to the roots by the death of a child," he warns. "These marriages can survive if the parents pull together . . . . If the marriage is shaky, or if one of the parents starts blaming the other for what has happened, your marriage is going to be in severe straits."[5]

Even when the child does not die but is developmentally disabled or chronically ill, Dr. Reuben advises parents to protect their marriage "Don't start blaming your spouse for what happened. And don't let others outside the marriage blame you, either. My sister had a congenitally deaf child after a pregnancy in which she took medication that her obstetrician prescribed. Her mother-in-law started blaming her for the child's deafness, and that caused severe problems in the marriage that eventually ended in divorce."[6]

While it is a normal part of grieving, anger can be harmful if it is suppressed. Granger Westberg says "resentment is not a healthy emotion and, if allowed to take over, it can be very, very harmful. Yet it is a normal part of the grief process. It is to be expected, it is to be wrestled with, and it can, by the grace of God, be overcome."[7]

After losing a treasure, we are often critical of everyone who had anything to do with the loss; we try to assign blame. We may rage at doctors who did or didn't operate, firemen who arrived too late, or God who allowed it to happen. We may also be angry with the loved one who died and so abandoned us.

9. *Resistance.* Somewhere in working through grief, we may become reluctant to return to normal living. People seem to have forgotten our tragedy, and we feel someone must keep the memory alive. Also, while grieving is painful, facing the changes our loss brings can be even more painful; and we want to stay with the now-familiar grief patterns.

Modern Western society no longer gives formal recognition to bereaved people. Relatives of the deceased used to wear black clothing for a year. Later, black armbands symbolized a recent loss. Today, once the funeral is over, one is expected to get on with life and forget the past.

Those who are not finished with grief often resent this attitude.

10. *Hope.* Since no two people are the same, the timetable for the appearance of hope is never the same either. But at some point, even after months of deep grief, the person will notice the loss was forgotten for a short time. They may laugh more. That life may return to something approaching normalcy now seems a possibility.

11. *Recovery.* Recovery means:
- feeling better.
- claiming your circumstances instead of your circumstances claiming your happiness.
- finding new meaning for living without the fear of future abandonment.
- enjoying fond memories without having them trigger painful feelings of loss, guilt, regret, or remorse.
- acknowledging it is all right to feel bad from time to time and to talk about those feelings no matter how those around you react.
- forgiving others when they say or do things that you

Who Says Winners Never Lose?

know are based on their lack of knowledge about grief.

- realizing that your ability to talk about the loss you've experienced is in fact helping another person get through his or her loss.[8]

Life will never be exactly as it was before the loss, but the final stage of grief is acceptance and continuing on with life. When we work through the process in a healthy manner, we realize we have not lost everything. We can never lose God, and we nearly always have many other blessings to comfort us.

Again, these steps are a general pattern of grief, observed in victims of loss. You may experience some of them out of sequence or even several at a time.

A person can deny, and at the next moment feel angry, and also have a constant, pervasive sense of guilt. You can almost simultaneously forget that your father isn't going to go to the baseball game with you, feel angry with him, and feel guilty about being angry. Our emotions work in subtle, fluid, complex ways. They certainly don't line up in an orderly, neat, conscious way. All these feelings are "normal."[9]

When Bill and Doreen Dolleman's son, Jason, was stillborn, they experienced society's unfamiliarity with the needs of grievers. "We were devastated," Bill said. "For many long months, we suffered alone, isolated from our family and friends, because no one really understood or knew how to reach out to us. We had a desperate need to talk about our experience and the problems we were having in dealing with our loss, and yet no one was there for us. Many people actually avoided us. Our phone was strangely silent for several months and only one friend asked me to tell them what had happened.

Climbing the Steep Trail Out

"Some comments that did filter back to us inferred that it must have been a lack of faith on our part that caused this tragedy in our lives; that we should be joyful and not grieving over our son's death; that we were lucky to already have two healthy children, and we could always have more!

"These comments hurt us so much. What we really needed most was people who would just listen, let us share our feelings and frustrations, and cry with us."

Remember that everyone grieves uniquely—we should never judge the quality of another's grief by comparing their reaction to ours. Also remember that we are never the same after loss. A scar remains.

Even if no one else understands our struggle through the grief process, we may look to God for comfort. "As a mother comforts her child, so will I comfort you" (Isa. 66:13).

TIME TO CONSIDER

1. Which steps in the process of grieving have you experienced? What was your loss?

2. Describe what stage(s) of grief were most difficult and why. How did you work through them?

3. How did God, a spouse, or a friend meet some of your needs at this time? Did others respond to you in a hurtful way—giving advice, judging, etc.? How did it cause you to feel?

4. What have you learned through your own grief process that might enable you to comfort another in their time of grief?

11

Nursing Our Wounds

Time alone does not heal. If wounds are not properly cleansed and dressed, time can cause them to fester and even kill. This is true for emotional wounds as well as physical ones.

If wounds we receive in our fall are given the wrong treatment, they become infected and prevent recovery.

THE WRONG TREATMENT

We are taught to deal with loss by *suppressing our feelings*. We grow up hearing, "You'll feel better soon." "Big boys like you don't cry." "Don't feel sad. She's in a much better place."

In our culture, men learn it's unmasculine to cry. Many think tears are a sign of weakness; and if they let themselves go, they'll lose control and have a nervous

Who Says Winners Never Lose?

breakdown. In reality, the danger comes from bottling up one's emotions.

Christians may feel weeping displays a lack of trust in the sovereignty of God because Paul said, "We do not want you to . . . grieve like the rest of men, who have no hope" (1 Thess. 4:13).

Grief is a normal part of human nature. God made tear ducts for a purpose. He expects us to use them when appropriate. To say faith relieves our need to work through the grief process is not only unrealistic, it is unscriptural. The "stiff upper lip" philosophy came from the followers of Stoicism, not Christianity. Stoics believed that putting aside passion was one of the disciplines necessary to attain true freedom and rule over one's own life.

Scripture, in fact, records many instances of men and women who grieved over loss. The patriarch Abraham wept when Sarah died (Gen. 23:2).

Even though they were tramping around in the desert, the Israelites set aside thirty days to mourn Aaron's death (Num. 20:29). They later "grieved for Moses in the plains of Moab thirty days, until the time of weeping and mourning was over" (Deut. 34:8).

When the tribe of Benjamin faced extinction, the rest of the Israelites "sat before God until evening, raising their voices and weeping bitterly" (Judg. 21:2).

When King Saul and his son Jonathan were killed, David and all the valiant soldiers "mourned and wept and fasted" (2 Sam. 1:12).

Surrounded by weeping soldiers at Abner's burial, David wept aloud, sang a lament, then refused to eat for the rest of the day (2 Sam. 3:32–35). He wept when his infant son was ill (12:21) and when he received news of his son Absalom's death (18:33).

Mary and Martha wept for their brother Lazarus even

though they knew he would "rise again in the resurrection at the last day" (John 11:24). When Dorcas died, her friends cried openly in front of Peter (Acts 9:39).

Scripture teaches us to grieve. We are not to grieve in the same way as people without hope, but we are certainly to grieve over loss.

Another unhealthy method of dealing with loss is *replacement*. "We'll get you another goldfish." "You can buy another car." "You can always have more children."

Unfortunately, a new pet is no comfort if the bereaved person is not ready to accept it. Any bereaved parent will tell you a lost child is irreplaceable, no matter how many other children they may have. If replacement is a good way to deal with all loss, what do we do at the loss of a grandparent—or loss of eyesight?

Scripture does not teach replacement for non-material losses. Job did not seek to replace his losses but shaved his head and tore his robe in the mourning ritual of the day. He blessed the name of the Lord who had taken it all away. God eventually blessed Job doubly, but Job did not substitute the mourning process with replacement.

The prodigal son's father did not adopt another son. He watched for a time of reunion with the young man (Luke 15:20).

A third faulty method of dealing with loss is believing *time heals all wounds*. When Jacob was told Joseph had been devoured by an animal, he put on sackcloth, mourned many days, and refused his family's attempts at comfort. "In mourning will I go down to the grave to my son," he said (Gen. 37:35).

Thirteen years later, Jacob had not recovered sufficiently from the loss of his beloved son to allow his youngest son out of his sight. When his oldest sons returned from buying grain and reported that Joseph was alive and ruling in

Who Says Winners Never Lose?

Egypt, he refused to believe it. Not until Jacob saw the carts Joseph had sent with his brothers to carry him back did his spirit revive. Time alone had not healed Jacob's grief.

"Time helps you adjust to the things around you," one bereaved mother says. "Time does not make the pain go away. The pain is still acute months, years later. The only difference is that we are capable of adjusting and learning to live with it. You learn to do things differently."[1]

Keeping busy is a fourth method people use to cope with grief. Grief in biblical times was expressed by setting aside normal activity, tearing the hair and clothes, beating the breast, and weeping and crying aloud.

While moping in a corner does not speed the healing process, neither does the common advice, *just keep busy*.

CLEARING UP THE INFECTION

Whenever the poison of unforgiveness is present, it will prevent total recovery. Resentment and anger toward ourselves, others, or God must be dealt with before we can regain strength to continue up the steps of the grief process.

Ourselves

We may know God and others have forgiven us for wrongdoing, but we may still be haunted by the memory of our failure. Guilt coils around us, pouring sludge and filth into our open wounds. Until we can banish this source of contamination, we will not get better.

David Seamands explains self-forgiveness from a fresh perspective:

> So many Christians say, "Yes, I know that God has forgiven me, but I can never forgive myself." This statement is a contradiction in terms. How can you really believe that God has forgiven you, and then not

Nursing Our Wounds

forgive yourself? When God forgives, He buries your sins in the sea of His forgiveness and His forgetfulness. As Corrie ten Boom says, "He then puts a sign on the bank which says, 'no fishing allowed.'" You have no right to dredge up anything that God has forgiven and forgotten. He has put it behind His back. Through an inscrutable mystery, divine omniscience has somehow forgotten your sins. You *can* forgive yourself.[2]

Others

Jesus had strong words about forgiving other people. "If you forgive men when they sin against you, your heavenly Father will also forgive you. But if you do not forgive men their sins, your Father will not forgive your sins" (Matt. 6:14,15).

When Peter asked how many times he should forgive his brother, Jesus told him "seventy-seven times" and illustrated it with the parable of the servant who would not forgive and landed in jail for his lack of mercy (Matt. 18:21–35).

God

Some people believe God owes them blessings and protection in return for their faith, allegiance, and tithes. When it's their turn to plunge into the pit of loss, they are shocked. *How can God do this to me? What is the use of ever trusting him again?*

Christians find it difficult to admit that they are angry with God. Many months passed before I admitted to myself I was mad at God, and years passed before I breathed the possibility to a close friend.

Facing resentment toward God is a major step in recovery. As with all forgiveness, we have the power to choose

Who Says Winners Never Lose?

to forgive whether or not we feel like it.

People in loss often feel as if God is waiting to bash them again with another painful loss. When we glimpse his overwhelming love for us and understand that every hurtful thing we go through causes him pain even when he allows it for a higher purpose, we can let go of our bitterness.

THE TWO PATHS

When Jim Conway's daughter lost her leg, Jim became aware that he faced only two choices.

> The one choice was I could be angry at God and I could follow the path of despair that I'd been going on. *Where were you God? I'm mad at you!* But that was only despair.
>
> The other choice I had was to let God be God and to say, "I don't know how all this fits together, I don't know the reason, I'm not even going to ask for reasons, but you are God and I'm the servant instead of me being God and you being the servant."
>
> What I'd been wrestling with was either God didn't care about me and Becky, or he was unable to care. Either one is devastating to your theology. But I came to see that neither of those were right. It wasn't that he was unable to care or that he didn't care, but I came to see that he had a higher purpose that I don't see altogether yet.
>
> Job said, "Even though he slays me I'm going to trust him." What really is involved is to make a choice.... It's either despair or it's God. There's nothing in-between.[3]

The prophet Habakkuk had a choice about his response to loss. He chose to praise God. "Even though the fig trees are all destroyed, and there is neither blossom left nor fruit, and though the olive crops all fail, and the fields lie barren; even if the flocks die in the fields and the cattle barns are empty, yet I will rejoice in the Lord; I will be happy in the God of my salvation" (Hab. 3:17,18 TLB).

Those bogged down in grief often talk of nothing but the loss. They may grow preoccupied with thoughts of suicide. Other danger signals are major weight change, insomnia, frequent bursting into tears, social isolation, growing use of alcohol and drugs, loss of sexual desire, and chronic fatigue. Usually one symptom is not cause for worry—some are normal at a particular stage in the grief process—but a combination indicates that the person should seek counsel.

TREATING THE WOUNDS OF OTHERS

The path of recovery not only leads to productive living for ourselves, but it is lined with opportunities for helping others.

A year after their son was stillborn, Bill and Doreen Dolleman began a support group for "forgotten parents"—those experiencing the loss of a baby at birth.

"Slowly, a healing process began in our lives as we began to meet with other parents, talk about our losses, and learn that our feelings were normal," Doreen said. "As time went on, we were able to reach out to others. Eventually we helped bring about many positive changes in educating health professionals and the public in how to meet the needs of grieving parents."

The support group, called P.S. My Baby Died (Parents of Stillborn), ministers to those who have suffered a miscarriage, stillbirth, or neonatal death. They offer monthly meetings, pamphlets, a lending library, newsletters, and "parent packets" that are distributed through doctors and hospitals. Parents who have experienced loss make

Who Says Winners Never Lose?

hospital visits, spend countless hours on the phone listening to grieving parents, and provide educational programs.

"Our little son, although we never really knew him, has enriched and blessed our lives and changed us in more ways than we would have ever thought possible," said Doreen. "With the passing of time, we learned just how faithful God is to keep his promises."

Although grief is experienced privately and uniquely, grievers know that those who have also suffered loss are the best comforters of all.

Paul points out that God "comforts us in all our troubles, so that we can comfort those in any trouble with the comfort we ourselves have received from God" (2 Cor. 1:4).

"Only to the extent that we ourselves have been comforted and encouraged by the Holy Spirit through His Word will we be able to comfort and encourage others," insists Jerry Bridges. "Adversity in our own lives, rightly responded to, enables us to be instruments of comfort and encouragement to others."[4]

We cannot always control our losses, but we can control our responses. Instead of focusing on what we have lost, let us thank God for what has not been taken, for what may be added to us in the future, and for opportunities to help others. This is the surest way to the healing of our wounds.

When we allow him to, God takes an active part in our recovery. "He heals the brokenhearted and binds up their wounds" (Ps. 147:3).

TIME TO CONSIDER

1. Four unhealthy responses to grief are to:
   - suppress our feelings
   - replace what was lost
   - expect time to heal all wounds
   - keep busy

If you have ever responded to loss in one or more of these ways, describe how it helped or hindered your grieving process.

2. Lack of forgiveness prevents recovery from loss. What steps help one move from unforgiveness to a refreshing, healing forgiveness? What part does God play in these steps?

3. Loss allows us to empathize with the loss of others. How have you or how might you in the future minister to others who are grieving?

12

Discovering the Gold

Once we negotiate the steep ascent of the grief process, cleanse our wounds so they can heal, and lend a hand to other wounded travelers, we should turn our pockets inside out and take inventory.

You see, as we fell into the canyon, little stones were dislodged. In the confusion of the fall and losing our treasure, we didn't notice the stones tumble into our pockets. As we began to climb the cliff, they rubbed together, rough edges grating against sharp corners, and slowly the stones' covering sifted away.

When we pull out the stones at the top, sun reflects off now-polished gold nuggets, and we discover that our loss has turned to gain.

Who Says Winners Never Lose?

MORE PRECIOUS THAN GOLD

Proverbs tells us about something even more desirable than gold.

> Blessed is the man who finds wisdom, the man who gains understanding, for she is more profitable than silver and yields better returns than gold. She is more precious than rubies; nothing you desire can compare with her. Long life is in her right hand; in her left hand are riches and honor. Her ways are pleasant ways, and all her paths are peace (Prov. 3:13–17).

Suppose you were reading the local university's catalog and came across this class description: *A practical course in wise living. Topics for discussion and lecture include: how to handle disappointments and tragedy; how to view life in proper perspective; how to comfort hurting people. Textbook required. 5 credits.*

Would you register? Guess what? You are already well into the semester. Experiencing loss is a great way to learn wisdom—one God employs all the time.

In chapter four, we saw that two of the reasons God allows loss in our lives are that loss reveals our need for God and loss tests us. Three of the reasons are nuggets of wisdom we may keep when we climb out of the canyon: the nugget of learning, the nugget of losing in order to gain, and the nugget of godliness.

The Nugget of Learning

1. *Learning how to handle future losses.* Each successive loss is not necessarily easier to bear in the sense that fresh losses remind us of former ones, yet we know better how to begin the grief process. We do not panic when we feel shock or depression or anger.

Discovering the Gold

We also learn the practical aspects of coping with loss. An automobile accident gave Marilyn top-notch training in how to contact authorities, fill out insurance forms, deal with emergency room personnel, and apply for sick leave. While she hopes she never has to go through the experience again, she now possesses the skills to handle a similar ordeal quickly and confidently.

2. *Learning perspective.* I never thought about heaven much until it became my son's new home. Now that I was keenly aware of the brevity of life, becoming a success no longer seemed so important. I gained new perspective on the importance of preparing for eternity, and I began to long for Christ's return as scripture says we should.

3. *Learning skills in comforting.* No one understands loss like one who's been there. A griever is painfully aware when a comforter has no inkling how loss feels. When we have suffered loss, we can draw on our own experiences to minister to hurting people.

Sometimes we want to comfort someone in a loss we have not experienced ourselves. When we don't know what to do or say, it may seem easier to avoid the hurting person, but that adds to their loss.

SUGGESTIONS FOR OFFERING COMFORT

Two of the most common losses are illness and bereavement. Following these suggestions can make a hospital or sick room visit a positive one.

1. *Be natural.* Just be yourself. The patient doesn't want to feel that his or her illness is making you uncomfortable.

2. *Be brief.* People who suffer from pain, fatigue, or fever cannot enjoy long visits. Ten minutes is plenty of time to reassure them of your love and concern. When patients play host and converse for much longer, they tire out.

Who Says Winners Never Lose?

3. *Don't hurry*. Standing gives the impression that you are anxious to leave. Sit on a chair (not the bed) during your visit.

4. *Be a listener*. The sick person is surrounded with busy nurses and doctors who do not have time for casual conversation. Don't talk about yourself the whole time.

5. *Allow the patient to bring up the subject of sickness*. You can open the door by asking vague questions such as "How are you doing today?" If the person doesn't want to talk about it, don't force the issue.

6. *Welcome serious conversation when the patient brings it up*. He or she may have thought a long time about talking with you about a difficult subject.

7. *Don't talk about the sick person to others within earshot*. It will make the person feel like an object.

For those who have a desire to help people in deep grief but have not yet experienced the loss themselves or were too busy recovering to take notes, here are a few suggestions from grief counselors.

8. *Make the first move*. People always say "If there's anything I can do, just call," but those in grief don't want to impose.

Call frequently and ask how they're doing. Listen to their answer. Ask them to lunch. Put significant anniversary dates on your calendar (birthdays, wedding anniversary, Christmas, anniversary of the death) and send cards or call on those days.

9. *Be careful you don't suggest incorrect methods of dealing with grief:* "suppress your feelings," "replace your loss," "time heals all wounds," or "just keep busy."

10. *Don't say* "I know just how you feel," "You should be grateful you had them for so long," "God must really love you to allow you to suffer so much," or quote the verse, "All things work together for good."

Discovering the Gold

11. *Don't even think of saying,* "You must not have had enough faith," or "There must be sin in your life."

12. *Periodically ask about the loss.* Ignoring it does not help the person in grief to forget, it only makes them feel you think their loss was unimportant. They have a need to talk about it, and one of the most helpful things you can do is listen.

13. *Whatever you say, don't use a "you poor thing" tone of voice.* Sympathy is welcome; pity is not.

The Nugget of Losing in Order to Gain

When Ahab became king of Israel, he not only married a foreigner, the Sidonian princess, Jezebel, but he built a temple to her god, Baal, and joined her in worship. He "did more to provoke the Lord, the God of Israel, to anger than did all the kings of Israel before him" (1 Kings 16:33).

The Lord sent his prophet, Elijah, to inform Ahab that, as punishment, God was sending a severe drought in the land. Knowing Ahab would take out his anger on Elijah, the Lord told Elijah to hide in the Kerith Ravine.

Now this was the life! Except for a little excitement once in a while, who could ask for anything more? He was safe from Ahab, with ravens bringing him food twice a day. He had running water for drinking and washing and no rain to dampen his comfort.

Then the brook dried up.

Had the stream continued to flow, Elijah might have stayed the rest of his life. No worries, no losses, and no risks. But as soon as the last puddle of water soaked into the thirsty ground, the Lord told Elijah to go to Queen Jezebel's home country, Sidon. "I have commanded a widow in that place to supply you with food," the Lord said (1 Kings 17:9).

What a plan. Ahab would never think of looking for the

Who Says Winners Never Lose?

prophet of God in a heathen land—especially at the home of a single woman.

At first glance, we might think that God was playing a little joke on Elijah. This woman was supposed to feed Elijah, yet when he asked for a piece of bread, she informed him that she had barely enough for a final meal for herself and her son before they starved to death.

This desperate state of affairs was the setting for another miracle of God. Elijah told her to go ahead and make him some bread, then feed herself and her son. "The jar of flour will not be used up and the jug of oil will not run dry until the day the Lord gives rain on the land," he said (1 Kings 17:14).

In spite of the monotonous cuisine, things continued smoothly until some time later when the boy became ill and died. When God raised him back to life at Elijah's earnest prayer, the mother's first recorded words were, "Now I know that you are a man of God and that the word of the Lord from your mouth is the truth" (1 Kings 17:24).

This story describes three losses that needed to happen before the people involved could receive greater gain.

LOSS	GAIN
1. Elijah was not safe in his own home	1. He received divine protection and care in the Kerith Ravine
2. The brook dried up	2. God performed the miracle of the continuing flour and oil that saved the lives of the widow, her son, and Elijah
3. The son died	3. The boy's resurrection convinced the woman of Elijah's authenticity and the truth of God's word

Discovering the Gold

We rarely see the potential for gain at the moment of our loss. Sometimes we never see it in this life. But nearly always, loss means a nugget of gain at the top of the path of recovery.

The Nugget of Godliness

Look at the life of any great man or woman of God, and you will find loss. In the case of leaders in the Bible, it was often the loss of loved ones.

Moses was separated from his natural family while growing up, then from all his people when he ran from the law for forty years. As a result, God developed in him the qualities he would need to lead several million newly freed slaves across the desert.

Enemy soldiers snatched Daniel from his family while he was still in his teens. Quickly learning to rely on God for wisdom and strength, he eventually became the prime minister of his adopted kingdom.

Esther, also living in exile, was orphaned at an early age and raised by a cousin. Becoming queen gave her the opportunity to save her people from slaughter, but the qualities she learned in adversity were what gave her courage to risk her life to do it.

NUGGETS FOR GOD

Among the gold in our hand is a nugget that God reserves to bring great spiritual blessing to many people.

As the story of missionary Jay Tucker's murder circulated around the world in articles, a film, and a book by his widow, many puzzled why God had allowed such a dedicated servant of God to be martyred. *What a waste!* they thought.

Twenty-one years later, they learned the rest of the story.

The Mangbetu tribe in Nganga was very resistant to

Who Says Winners Never Lose?

the gospel. Pioneer missionary C.T. Studd labored there without converts, then turned the area over to another mission which, through the decades, had no better success.

As the Congo rebellion subsided, the chief at Nganga asked a policeman called "the Brigadier" to become the chief of his police department. The Brigadier had accepted Christ through the ministry of Jay Tucker while living in the city of Isiro. He told the Mangbetus about the Savior he had found through the missionary whose body had been thrown into "their" river and whose blood had flowed through "their" waters.

The Mangbetus consider the land and rivers where they live to be theirs personally. Since Jay Tucker had been thrown into their water, they had to listen. What had seemed such a waste now became the key to their hearts, and they began to accept Christ.

Soon the Brigadier requested that the church at Isiro send pastors and evangelists to minister to the Christians and witness to the others. A great revival broke out and today thousands of converts live in Nganga. Among the Mangbetu tribe alone thirty churches belong to Jay Tucker's missionary organization.

Many times, people's effective ministry grows out of deep loss in their lives. Charles Colson's dynamic outreach to prisoners began with his loss of freedom after Watergate. Joni Eareckson Tada's paralysis laid the foundation for her fruitful ministry with the disabled. Dave Roever's incredible testimony of survival from a grenade explosion is the basis of his successful work with teens and Vietnam veterans. Corrie ten Boom's experiences during the holocaust made it possible for her to preach the gospel all over the world.

Scripture points out that a difficult experience never "seems pleasant at the time, but painful. Later on, however,

Discovering the Gold

it produces a harvest of righteousness and peace for those who have been trained by it" (Heb. 12:11).

Jesus emphasized that we must lose in order to gain spiritually. "Whoever wants to save his life will lose it, but whoever loses his life for me will save it. What good is it for a man to gain the whole world, and yet lose or forfeit his very self?" (Luke 9:24,25).

This message is so important that all four gospel writers recorded it. In fact, Matthew records Jesus saying it on two separate occasions (Matt. 10:39; 16:25; Mark 8:35; John 12:25).

Inherent in every loss is the potential for gain. It all depends on our attitude. "We . . . can choose to make grief a gift," says one counselor. "Within every loss there are seeds for gain and new beginnings."[1]

TIME TO CONSIDER

1. Discuss helpful things people said or did when you suffered loss.

2. The three nuggets of wisdom we discover through loss are:
- the nugget of learning
- the nugget of losing in order to gain
- the nugget of godliness

If you've discovered one of these nuggets, describe how it came about and how it has helped you grow.

13

Resuming the Journey

Insurance money may replace a home; we may recover from illness; a runaway son or daughter may return home. In such cases, although we bear scars from our trials, we find comfort in what has been restored.

Job experienced complete restoration in each of the areas he had lost. He had once been the East's richest man. Now God gave him twice as much—fourteen hundred sheep, six thousand camels, one thousand yoke of oxen, and one thousand donkeys.

Job's wife was given the opportunity of going through the pangs and joys of childbirth another ten times. While lost children can never be replaced, Job and his wife no longer suffered the stigma of childlessness. Also, when all were reunited in heaven, they would have twice as many children as before.

Who Says Winners Never Lose?

Not only did Job recover from the disease that caused his boils, he lived another one hundred forty years.

People no longer shunned Job. His relatives and "everyone who had known him before came and ate with him in his house. They comforted and consoled him over all the trouble the Lord had brought upon him, and each one gave him a piece of silver and a gold ring" (Job 42:11).

James writes about Job as an example of perseverance (James 5:11).

Job never completely lost his faith, but he was bewildered at the ways of God. Although he did not learn the reasons for his trial, it was enough that God was no longer hidden. "My ears had heard of you but now my eyes have seen you," Job said (42:5). The knowledge that God was able to do all things satisfied him (42:2).

Job's wife regained possessions, loved ones, and her husband's health. Since she was once again well-to-do, a mother, and a hostess of many people in the home, we can assume her contemporaries grew to respect her, although her position in history is another matter.

Since I have compassion for this woman who lost so much, I would like to believe she regretted her infamous outburst and sought reconciliation with God, even though scripture does not say. Surely Job shared with her what he learned when he met God face-to-face. Knowing that the mercy of God gave her back a healthy husband, children, double wealth, and many friends and visitors, she could dare to believe once more in his love and care.

We must be careful not to think that Job earned his blessings as a result of patience. James reminds us that God was not bound to replace Job's losses. God blessed Job because "the Lord is full of compassion and mercy" (James 5:11). This happy ending indicates that at times God does restore to us our losses. He enjoys showing us mercy.

RESTORATION IN FUTURE LIFE

We may know people whose lives seem little more than a collection of disappointments and tragedies—their losses outweighing their few gains. If they are Christians, however, their opportunity for restoration does not end at the grave.

Paul reminds us that "if we endure, we will also reign with him" (2 Tim. 2:12). Jesus more than restores our losses when we go to be with him. The sick will enjoy robust health, the fearful will be confident, the weeping will be joyful, the bereaved will never again face death, and the victims of unfaithful spouses will be united forever with the faithful Bridegroom.

Earthly life is not the end. When our losses are not restored to us here or are late in coming, we can follow the example of Jesus "who for the joy set before him endured" (Heb. 12:2).

JESUS' IDENTIFICATION WITH US

Jesus always understands our losses. He left the splendor and comfort of heaven to rescue mankind from Satan's clutches. Through a divine miracle, he became a fetus in the womb of a virgin. From that moment on, he experienced life as a mortal. During his short life, he suffered loss in the same five areas we do.

1. *Possessions.* The Bible tells us that among heaven's treasures are pearl gates, streets of gold, and walls of precious stones. Jesus left it all to join a carpenter's family. Although Joseph's profession was honorable, it provided only necessities. When Mary came to the temple for her purification after giving birth to Jesus, she brought the sacrifice prescribed for poor people (Lev. 12:8, Luke 2:24).

As an adult, Jesus said, "Foxes have holes and birds of the air have nests, but the Son of Man has no place to lay

Who Says Winners Never Lose?

his head" (Luke 9:58). When the temple tax came due, Jesus did not have the money. He asked Peter to catch a fish and take a four-drachma coin from its mouth to pay the tax for them both (Matt. 17:27).

John tells us that Judas "was a thief; as keeper of the money bag, he used to help himself to what was put into it" (John 12:6). This was money that all the disciples, including Jesus, needed for basic necessities.

2. *Loved ones.* Mary spent the early months of her pregnancy with her relative, Elizabeth. Their sons—Jesus and John—were born just months apart.

As an adult, John the Baptist prepared the way for Jesus' public ministry. When the outspoken John accused Herod of evil deeds, the ruler threw him in prison and later had him beheaded.

This loss so affected Jesus that "when Jesus heard what had happened, he withdrew by boat privately to a solitary place" (Matt. 14:13). He had raised others from the dead but it was not God's plan that he should raise his beloved relative.

Jesus was saddened by the grief Lazarus' death had caused Mary and Martha even though he knew he would soon bring Lazarus back to life. "When Jesus saw [Mary] weeping, and the Jews who had come along with her also weeping, he was deeply moved in spirit and troubled. 'Where have you laid him?' he asked. 'Come and see, Lord,' they replied. Jesus wept. Then the Jews said, 'See how he loved him!'" (John 11:33–36). Approaching the tomb, he was "once more deeply moved" (11:38).

3. *Health.* Following the last supper, Jesus spent a sleepless night praying in the garden of Gethsemane. Knowing what he would soon face, he told his disciples, "My soul is overwhelmed with sorrow to the point of death" (Matt. 26:38).

Resuming the Journey

Luke, the physician of the group, is the only gospel writer to mention that as Jesus prayed, "his sweat was like drops of blood falling to the ground" (Luke 22:44). In this rare phenomenon of *hematidrosis,* great emotional strain causes tiny capillaries in the sweat glands to rupture, mixing blood with sweat.

The ruptured capillaries sensitize the skin similarly to a second degree sunburn. After his arrest, soldiers struck Jesus repeatedly in his tender face. He suffered bruises, possibly a broken nose, and probably a concussion, producing headache, dizziness, and shock.

Jesus was then stripped of all clothes, tied to a post, and whipped with a flagrum made of leather strips embedded with sheep knuckles or lead balls. The blows produced deep bruises and cuts leaving quivering ribbons of bleeding flesh.

The soldiers twisted long, double-barbed thorns into the shape of a crown and pressed it on his head. They draped a purple robe on his mutilated back, again hit him on the head and face. "Hail, king of the Jews!" they mocked. Tired of their sport, they tore the robe from his back, reopening wounds that had stuck to the cloth.

An article in the Journal of the American Medical Association states, "The physical and mental abuse . . . as well as the lack of food, water, and sleep, also contributed to his generally weakened state. Therefore, even before the actual crucifixion, Jesus' physical condition was at least serious and possibly critical."[1]

As Jesus was forced to carry his own cross to the site of crucifixion, the weight of the wooden beam (about 150 lbs.), pain from the rough wood gouging his lacerated skin and muscles, along with the shock from copious blood loss, caused him to collapse on the road.

Jesus' hands (or wrist area) and feet were nailed to the

cross with square, iron nails that crushed nerves in his wrists and feet. Stretched on the wooden beams, movement from his neck down was limited, giving the effect of paralysis without the benefit of numbness.

He first experienced fiery pain in his limbs, then great waves of cramps knotted the muscles in throbbing agony. As his chest muscles became paralyzed and the muscles near his ribs could not function, he fought to raise himself up on nailed feet to expel air from his lungs. With each breath, tissue was torn from his lacerated back as he moved up and down against the rough timber.

Finally Jesus experienced a crushing pain deep in his chest as the sac around his heart slowly filled with serum. As one doctor explains, "It is now almost over—the loss of tissue fluid has reached a critical level—the compressed heart is struggling to pump heavy, thick sluggish blood into the tissues—the tortured lungs are making a frantic effort to gasp in small gulps of air."[2]

Most experts agree the final cause of death was either suffocation or heart failure. Not by chance does the English word "excruciating" come from the Latin *excruciatus*, which means "out of the cross." A more painful death can scarcely be imagined.

My purpose in including these details is to point out how completely Jesus can identify with us when we suffer physically. He experienced pain in every part of the body; his symptoms were similar to those of asthma, heart disease, Amytrophic Lateral Sclerosis (Lou Gerhig's disease), and migraines. He can identify with victims of burns, lacerations, beatings, suffocation, torture.

4. *Dignity and other intangibles.* All the health losses Jesus suffered occurred at the end of his life, but his loss of dignity and other intangibles began at birth.

Jesus grew up with the stigma of illegitimacy. When he

Resuming the Journey

tried to minister in his hometown, the people asked, "Where did this man get this wisdom and these miraculous powers? ... Isn't this the carpenter's son? Isn't his mother's name Mary?" (Matt. 13:54,55). They were well acquainted with his family and the fact that Mary became pregnant before she was married. Few bought the notion that Jesus was virgin-born.

As he was dying, the chief priests, teachers of the law, and passers-by mocked him. " 'He saved others,' they said, 'but he can't save himself!' " (Mark 15:31). Even the thieves dying beside him joined in the taunts. For the sake of modesty, religious paintings depict a loin cloth around his waist during the crucifixion; but in reality, victims were usually stripped of all clothing.

Jesus experienced loss of favor when the Pharisees tried to trap him with trick questions, attributed his miracle-working power to the devil, and continually plotted to have him arrested and killed.

Jesus lost freedom when he was arrested by an unauthorized guard, given a hurried, illegal night trial, convicted on inadmissible testimony, then executed for a crime he did not commit.

The flogging, blows on the face and head, crown of thorns, and stresses of crucifixion disfigured his physical appearance.

Because he had subjected himself to the laws of nature, Jesus' power was limited while he was in a physical body. For example, he could not be in two places at once, breathe under water, nor go very long without eating or sleeping.

His work was often hampered by people's misunderstanding, jealousy, or lack of faith. As a result, he experienced frustration with the unrepentant cities (Matt. 11:20); with the Pharisees and teachers of the law (Matt. 15:3–9); with his disciples (Matt. 8:26);

especially Peter (Matt. 14:31); with the temple sellers (Matt. 21:12,13); and with his relatives' lack of faith (Mark 6:4–6).

Being sinless and perfect does not mean Jesus is unfamiliar with the loss of intangibles. As the prophet Isaiah pointed out, "He was despised and rejected by men, a man of sorrows, and familiar with suffering" (Isa. 53:3).

5. *Faith in God.* "About noon, darkness fell across the entire land, lasting until three o'clock that afternoon. Then Jesus called out with a loud voice, *'Eli, Eli, lama sabachthani?'* ('My God, my God, why have you deserted me?')" (Mark 15:33,34 TLB).

At that moment, Jesus, who had never committed a sin in his life, took on the sins of the world. We have no way to comprehend the shame, filth, and weight of that awful burden. Then, in Jesus' darkest hour, sin cut him off from the holy Father God and, for the first time ever, Jesus experienced the feelings of abandonment and isolation.

Jesus understands people who feel they have lost God.

ONE WHO UNDERSTANDS

As you read this book, you may be hurting so badly you see no reason to go on struggling. You don't know why you lost your treasure, your losses haven't been restored, and the promise of blessing in heaven seems far away.

On dark days such as this, remember Jesus understands. He is not "unable to sympathize with our weaknesses, but . . . has been tempted in every way, just as we are—yet was without sin" (Heb. 4:15). Whatever your loss, Jesus knows how you feel.

The good news is that, not only does Jesus understand our losses, he is able to do something about them. He rose from the dead and now "is able to save completely those who come to God through him, because he always lives to

Resuming the Journey

intercede for them" (Heb. 7:25). Because of this, scripture encourages us to "approach the throne of grace with confidence, so that we may receive mercy and find grace to help us in our time of need" (Heb. 4:16).

Jesus could have refused to go through with his trial and crucifixion. As he was being arrested, he told Peter, "Do you think I cannot call on my Father, and he will at once put at my disposal more than twelve legions of angels?" (Matt. 26:53).

Jesus was willing to go through his terrible agony because he loves us. There was no other way to rescue us from eternal punishment, so he took our place and paid for our sin. Such love cannot turn a calloused ear to our plight when we cry for relief.

Cling to this truth: "Weeping may remain for a night, but rejoicing comes in the morning" (Ps. 30:5). Hang on a while longer. God will never abandon you but will stay with you until darkness flees.

WHO SAYS WINNERS NEVER LOSE?

No one is immune from loss—not even the Son of God himself. Everyone plunges into the pit at one time or another, but each of us can choose to climb the steps out and resume life as changed people. With God's help, we will profit from life's painful detours.

TIME TO CONSIDER

1. If you have received restoration of a loss as Job did, describe it.

2. If you have not received restoration, do you feel angry, resolved, resentful? Why might God restore losses in one circumstance and not in another?

Who Says Winners Never Lose?

3. Describe some of Jesus' losses.

4. Since Jesus has suffered as we do, how might he comfort us?

Source Notes

Chapter 1

1. Ira J. Tanner, *The Gift of Grief* (New York: Hawthorn Books, Inc., 1976), p. 56.
2. The stigma of childlessness not only applied to barren women, but to women who had borne children who subsequently died. See 1 Samuel 15:33 and Jeremiah 15:8,9.
3. Harriet Sarnoff Schiff, *The Bereaved Parent* (New York: Penguin Books, 1978), p. 78.

Chapter 3

1. Thomas Thompson, *Lost!* (New York: Atheneum Publishers, 1975).
2. Philip Yancey, *Where Is God When It Hurts?* (Grand Rapids: Zondervan, 1977), pp. 71,72.

Who Says Winners Never Lose?

3. Richard Stengel, "It Was No Breeze," *Time*, September 26, 1988, p. 17.
4. Yancey, pp. 63,64.

Chapter 4

1. Philip Yancey, *Where Is God When It Hurts?* (Grand Rapids: Zondervan, 1977), pp. 66,67.
2. Harold S. Kushner, *When Bad Things Happen to Good People* (New York: Avon Books, 1983), p. 43.
3. Jerry Bridges, *Trusting God Even When Life Hurts* (Colorado Springs: NavPress, 1988), pp. 27,25.
4. Bert Ghezzi, "The Promise of Problems," *Pentecostal Evangel*, August 21, 1988, p. 6.
5. Bridges, p. 165.

Chapter 5

1. Tanner, p. 17.
2. Tanner, p. 3.
3. Corrie ten Boom, *The Hiding Place* (Old Tappan, NJ: Spire Books, Fleming H. Revell Company, 1971), p. 149.
4. Anthony Campolo, Jr., *The Success Fantasy* (Wheaton: Victor Books, 1982), p. 11.

Chapter 6

1. Ralph G. Turnbull, ed., *Baker's Dictionary of Practical Theology* (Grand Rapids: Baker Book House, 1967), p. 227.
2. Joan Bordow, *The Ultimate Loss: Coping with the Death of a Child* (New York: Beaufort Books, 1982), p. 17.
3. Nancy O'Conner, Ph.D., *Letting Go With Love: The Grieving Process* (Tucson, AZ: La Mariposa Press, 1984), pp. 78,79.

Source Notes

4. Granger E. Westberg, *Good Grief* (Philadelphia: Fortress Press, 1962, 1971), p. 14.
5. Tanner, p. 23.

Chapter 7

1. Simon S. Levin, *Adams' Rib: Essays on Biblical Medicine* (Los Altos, CA: Geron-X, Inc., 1970), p. 79. Dermatitis herpetiformis is a chronic skin disease marked by extensive patches of itching blisters and papules.
2. Barnes Notes, Vol 1, 116.
3. Irma Myers and Arthur Myers, *Why You Feel Down & What You Can Do About It* (New York: Atheneum Publishers, 1982), pp. 23,24.
4. T. H. Holmes and R. H. Rahe, "The Social Readjustment Rating Scale," *Journal of Psychosomatic Research* Vol. 11, 213–218.

Chapter 8

1. Susan Whitehead, "On Hold," *Today's Christian Woman,* July/August 1986, p. 40.
2. Brian Blair, "Through the Fire," *Charisma,* August 1986, pp. 43–46.
3. Dr. James Dobson, *Hide or Seek* (Old Tappan, NJ: Fleming H. Revell, 1974), p. 41.
4. Dave Roever, *Welcome Home, Davey* (Waco, TX: Word Books, 1986), p. 125.
5. Tanner, p. 14.

Chapter 9

1. Jim and Becky Conway, "Family In Crisis," *Focus on the Family*, KCIS, Seattle, WA, 21 March 1989. Radio Program.

Who Says Winners Never Lose?

2. Mervyn Rothstein, "Open-eyed look at Holocaust cost Jewish writer his faith," *The Herald*, January 22, 1989, sec. F5.
3. Joseph Parker, *Pathways to Happiness*, (as quoted in *Baker's Dictionary of Practical Theology*, Ralph G.Turnbull, ed. [Grand Rapids: Baker Book House, 1967], pp. 227,228.
4. Becky Smith Greer, "Surviving a Personal Loss," *Focus on the Family*, KCIS, Seattle, WA, 11 August 1986. Radio Program.
5. Sheldon Vanauken, *A Severe Mercy* (San Francisco: Harper & Row, 1977), pp. 190,191.
6. "Family In Crisis."

Chapter 10

1. Westberg, pp. 66–80.
2. Tanner, p. 70.
3. Turnbull, ed., p. 228.
4. Wonda Layton, "Mourning Has Broken," (unpublished manuscript), p. 61.
5. Judi Hunt, "The Loss of a Child Can Shake a Marriage," *Seattle Post-Intelligencer*, May 24, 1986, sec. D3.
6. "The Loss of a Child Can Shake a Marriage."
7. Westberg, p. 51.
8. John W. James and Frank Cherry, *The Grief Recovery Handbook* (New York: Harper & Row, 1988), p. 7.
9. Myers and Myers, p. 26.

Chapter 11

1. Katherine Fair Donnelly, *Recovering From the Loss of a Child* (New York: Macmillan, 1982), p. 38.
2. David A. Seamands, *Healing for Damaged Emotions* (Wheaton: Victor Books, 1981), p. 22.

3. "Family In Crisis."
4. Bridges, p. 188.

Chapter 12

1. Tanner, p. 167.

Chapter 13

1. William D. Edwards, M.D., Wesley J. Gabel, M.Div., Floyd E. Hosmer, M.S. A.M.I., "On the Physical Death of Jesus," *Journal of the American Medical Association,* Vol. 255, No. 11, March 21, 1986, 1455–1464.
2. C. Truman Davis, M.D., M.S., "The Crucifixion of Jesus," *Arizona Medicine,* Vol. 22, No. 3, March 1965.

Support Group Leader's Guide

Issue-oriented, problem-wrestling, life-confronting—Aglow Publication's Heart Issue books are appropriate for adult Sunday school classes, individual study, and especially for support groups. To encourage and facilitate support groups, Aglow Publications includes the following guidelines.

SUPPORT GROUP GUIDELINES

The small group setting offers individuals the opportunity to commit themselves to personal growth through mutual caring and support. This is especially true of Christian support groups, where from five to twelve individuals meet on a regular basis with a mature leader to share their personal experiences and struggles over a specific "heart issue." In such a group, individuals develop trust and

Who Says Winners Never Lose?

accountability with each other and the Lord. Because a support group's purpose differs from a Bible study or prayer group, it has its own format and guidelines.

Let's look at the ingredients of a support group:
- Purpose
- Leadership
- Meeting Format
- Group Guidelines

PURPOSE

The purpose of a Heart Issue support group is to provide:

1. An *opportunity* for participants to share openly and honestly their struggles and pain over a specific issue in a nonjudgmental Christ-centered framework.

2. A *"safe place"* where participants can gain perspective on a mutual problem and begin taking responsibility for their response to their own situation.

3. An *atmosphere* that is compassionate, understanding, and committed to challenging participants from a biblical perspective.

Support groups are not counseling groups. Participants come to be supported, not fixed or changed. Yet, as genuine love and caring are exchanged, they begin to experience God's love and acceptance. As a result, change and healing take place.

The initiators of a support group need to be clear about its specific purpose. The following questions are examples of what to consider before starting a small group.

1. What type of group will this be? A personal growth group, a self-help group, or a group structured to focus on a certain theme? Is it long-term, short-term, or ongoing?

2. Who is the group for? A particular population? College students? Single women? Divorced people?

3. What are the goals for the group? What will members gain from it?

4. Who will lead or co-lead this group? What are his/her qualifications?

5. How many members should be in the group? Will new members be able to join the group once it is started?

6. What kind of structure or format will the group have?

7. What topics will be explored in the support book and to what degree will this be determined by the group members and to what degree by the leaders?

LEADERSHIP

Small group studies often rotate leadership among participants, but because support groups usually meet for a specific time period with a specific mutual issue, it works well to have one leader or a team of co-leaders responsible for meetings.

Good leadership is essential for a healthy, balanced group. Qualifications include character and personality traits as well as life experience and, in some cases, professional experience.

Personal Leadership Characteristics

Courage

One of the most important personal traits of effective group leaders is courage. Courage is shown in willingness (1) to be open to self-disclose, admitting their own mistakes and taking the same risks they expect others to take; (2) to confront another, and, in confronting, to understand that love is the goal; (3) to act on their beliefs and hunches; (4) to be emotionally touched by another and to draw on their experiences in order to identify with the other; (5) to continually examine their inner self; (6) to be direct and honest with members; and (7) to express to the group their

Who Says Winners Never Lose?

fears and expectations about the group process. (Leaders shouldn't use their role to protect themselves from honest and direct interaction with the rest of the group.)

Willingness to Model

Through their behavior, and the attitudes conveyed by it, leaders can create a climate of openness, seriousness of purpose, acceptance of others, and the desirability of taking risks. Group leaders should have had some moderate victory in their own struggles, with adequate healing having taken place. They recognize their own woundedness and see themselves as persons in process as well. Group leaders lead largely by example—by doing what they expect members to do.

Presence

Group leaders need to be emotionally present with the group members. This means being touched by others' pain, struggles, and joys. Leaders can become more emotionally involved with others by paying close attention to their own reactions and by permitting these reactions to become intense. Fully experiencing emotions gives leaders the ability to be compassionate and empathetic with their members. At the same time, group leaders understand their role as facilitators. They know they're not answer people; they don't take responsibility for change in others.

Goodwill and Caring

A sincere interest in the welfare of the others is essential in group leaders. Caring involves respecting, trusting, and valuing people. Not every member is easy to care for, but leaders should at least want to care. It is vital that leaders become aware of the kinds of people they care for easily and the kinds they find it difficult to care for. They can gain

Support Group Leader's Guide

this awareness by openly exploring their reactions to members. Genuine caring must be demonstrated; merely saying so is not enough.

Some ways to express a caring attitude are: (1) inviting a person to participate but allowing that person to decide how far to go; (2) giving warmth, concern, and support when, and only when, it is genuinely felt; (3) gently confronting the person when there are obvious discrepancies between a person's words and her behavior; (4) encouraging people to be what they could be without their masks and shields. This kind of caring requires a commitment to love and a sensitivity to the Holy Spirit.

Openness

To be effective, group leaders must be open with themselves, open to others in groups, open to new experiences, and open to life-styles and values that differ from their own. Openness is an attitude. It doesn't mean that leaders reveal every aspect of their personal lives; it means that they reveal enough of themselves to give the participants a sense of person.

Leader openness tends to foster a spirit of openness within the group; it permits members to become more open about their feelings and beliefs; and it lends a certain fluidity to the group process. Self-revelation should not be manipulated as a technique. However, self-evaluation is best done spontaneously, when appropriate.

Nondefensiveness

Dealing frankly with criticism is related closely to openness. If group leaders are easily threatened, insecure in their work of leading, overly sensitive to negative feedback, and highly dependent on group approval, they will probably encounter major problems in trying to carry

Who Says Winners Never Lose?

out their leadership role. Members sometimes accuse leaders of not caring enough, of being selective in their caring, of structuring the sessions too much, of not providing enough direction, of being too harsh. Some criticism may be fair, some unfair. The crucial thing for leaders is to nondefensively explore with their groups the feelings that are legitimately produced by the leaders and those that represent what is upsetting the member.

Strong Sense of Self

A strong sense of self (or personal power) is an important quality of leaders. This doesn't mean that leaders would manipulate or dominate; it means that leaders are confident of who they are and what they are about. Groups "catch" this and feel the leaders know what they are doing. Leaders who have a strong sense of self recognize their weaknesses and don't expend energy concealing them from others. Their vulnerability becomes their strength as leaders. Such leaders can accept credit where it's due and, at the same time, encourage members to accept credit for their own growth.

Stamina

Group leading can be taxing and draining as well as exciting and energizing. Leaders need physical and emotional stamina and the ability to withstand pressure in order to remain vitalized until the group sessions end. If leaders give in to fatigue when the group bogs down, becomes resistive, or when members drop out, the effectiveness of the whole group could suffer. Leaders must be aware of their own energy level, have outside sources of spiritual and emotional nourishment, and have realistic expectations for the group's progress.

Sense of Humor

The leaders who enjoy humor and can incorporate it appropriately into the group will bring a valuable asset to the meetings. Sometimes humor surfaces as an escape from healthy confrontations and sensitive leaders need to identify and help the group avoid this diversion. But because we often take ourselves and our problems too seriously, we need the release of humor to bring balance and perspective. This is particularly true after sustained periods of dealing seriously with intensive problems.

Creativity

The capacity to be spontaneously creative, to approach each group session with fresh ideas is a most important characteristic for group leaders. Leaders who are good at discovering new ways of approaching a group and who are willing to suspend the use of established techniques are unlikely to grow stale. Working with interesting co-leaders is another way for leaders to acquire fresh ideas.

GROUP LEADERSHIP SKILLS

Although personality characteristics of the group leader are extremely significant, by themselves they do not ensure a healthy group. Leadership skills are also essential. The following need to be expressed in a sensitive and timely way:

Active Listening

Leaders need to absorb content, note gestures, observe subtle changes in voice or expression, and sense underlying messages. For example, a woman may be talking about her warm and loving feelings toward her husband, yet her body may be rigid and her fists clenched.

Who Says Winners Never Lose?

Empathy
This requires sensing the subjective world of the participant. Group leaders, in addition to being caring and open, must learn to grasp another's experience and at the same time maintain their separateness.

Respect and Positive Regard
In giving support, leaders need to draw on the positive assets of the members. Where differences occur, there needs to be open and honest appreciation and toleration.

Warmth
Smiling has been shown to be especially important in the communication of warmth. Other nonverbal means are voice tone, posture, body language, and facial expression.

Genuineness
Leaders need to be real, to be themselves in relating with others, to be authentic and spontaneous.

FORMAT

The format of meetings will differ vastly from group to group, but the following are generally accepted as working well with support groups.

Meeting Place
This should be a comfortable, warm atmosphere. Participants need to feel welcome and that they've come to a "safe place" where they won't be overheard or easily distracted. Some groups will want to provide baby-sitting.

Opening
Welcome participants. The leader should introduce herself and the members. It is wise to go over the "ground

Support Group Leader's Guide

rules" at every meeting, especially at first or when there are newcomers. Some of these would include:

1. Respect others' sharing by keeping what is said confidential.

2. Never belittle the beliefs or expressions of another.

3. Respect the time schedule. Arrive on time and be prompt in leaving.

4. Feel free to contact the leader at another time if you have questions or need additional help.

Many meetings open with a brief time of prayer and worship and conclude with prayer. It often helps to ask for informal prayer requests and brief sharing so that the group begins in a spirit of openness.

Meeting

Leaders can initiate the meeting by focusing on a particular issue (or chapter if the group is studying a book). It is wise to define the focus of the specific meeting so that the group can stay on track for the entire session. (See Group Guidelines below.)

Closing

Strive for promptness without being abrupt. Give an opportunity for those who need additional help to make an appointment with the leader. Be alert to those needing special affirmation or encouragement as they leave.

GROUP GUIDELINES

Because this is a support group, not an advice group, the leader will need to establish the atmosphere and show by her style how to relate lovingly and helpfully within the group. Participants need to know the guidelines for being a member of the group. It is a wise practice to repeat these guidelines at each meeting and especially when newcomers

Who Says Winners Never Lose?

attend. The following guidelines have proven to be helpful to share with support groups:

1. You have come to give and receive support. No "fixing." We are to listen, support, and be supported by one another—not give advice.

2. Let other members talk. Please let them finish without interruption.

3. Try to step over any fear of sharing in the group. Yet do not monopolize the group's time.

4. Be interested in what someone else is sharing. Listen with your heart. Never converse privately with someone else while another member is addressing the group.

5. Be committed to express your feelings from the heart. Encourage others to do the same. It's all right to feel angry, to laugh, or to cry.

6. Help others own their feelings and take responsibility for change in their lives. Don't jump in with an easy answer or a story on how you conquered their problem. Relate to where they are.

7. Avoid accusing or blaming. Speak in the "I" mode about how something or someone made *you* feel. Example: "I felt angry when . . . ."

8. Avoid ill-timed humor to lighten emotionally charged times. Let participants work through their sharing even if it is hard.

9. Keep names and sharing of other group members confidential.

10. Because we are all in various stages of growth, please give newcomers permission to be new and old-timers permission to be further along in their growth. This is a "safe place" for all to grow and share their lives.

Inquiries regarding speaking availability and other correspondence may be directed to Diana Kruger at the following address:

P.O. Box 59712
Renton, WA 98058